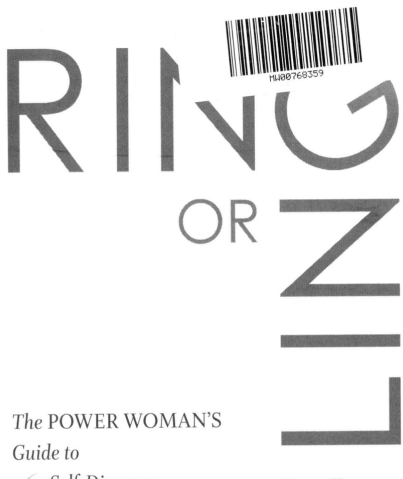

RING OR FLING

The POWER WOMAN'S
Guide to
✓ *Self-Discovery,*
✓ *Setting Standards, and*
✓ *Dating with Confidence*

CLAIRE BROWN

POWER WOMEN PRESS

Cover design by WildEagles'99 via 99Designs
Book design and production by Alex Head / Draft Lab

ISBN: 978-1-7347956-0-8

Printed in the United States of America
First Edition

For every woman who needs to discover—or rediscover—
the Power Woman within!

And for all who have contributed to my heartbreaks,
who have helped me heal during the breakdowns,
or who empowered me to have the breakthroughs
necessary to help others.

(Don't worry, I haven't told all the secrets!)

Contents

RING OR FLING

The Power of Knowing Who You Are and What You Want

When women have standards, they stand out. They are passionate, they are building successful careers, they know their value, they rely on their villages of other amazing women to lift them up and set them straight, and they're hotter than the Fourth of July—because they've got confidence rooted in their standards. When they are also single…well, that just makes them the total package.

Since you picked up this book, I'm going to assume you relate. You're a woman with standards for your work, your home, your appearance. You have standards in just about every area of your life. But let me ask you this: what are your standards for dating?

For many of us, the standards that make us rock stars in our daily lives don't extend to our dating lives. Many of us date by trial and error, without practicing self-care or taking the time to discover ourselves enough to learn what we truly want in a partner. And as a result, we find ourselves going on bad date after bad date with men who don't measure up to what we expect or deserve in our lives. After this continues for a while, it can be tempting to settle—accepting a man who isn't right simply to avoid being alone.

So, how do we find men who do measure up? In the book *Act*

Like a Lady, Think Like a Man, Steve Harvey spends an entire chapter telling women to get some standards, because it's so attractive to a man of quality for a woman to have values. When you care for yourself, set your standards, and stick to them, you become catnip to those "men of quality," right? Well, Steve, you may be right, but it's not quite that easy.

After I was in the Singlehood for a few years, I matched with a man from another state on a dating app. He was passing through my town, and as soon as we matched, he called me, curious about all things in my world. I always appreciate a conversation, because I need clarity and many times the men do too! Here's how this dialogue went:

Dude: Hey, Claire! Tell me about yourself!

Me: Well, I've been a real estate broker for over seventeen years, I run a women's platform, I launched a podcast, and I've written a book. For fun, I like to read, write, and ride my bike.

Dude: Wow! Ugh, that's all pretty intimidating!

This is followed by a long, intimidating silence. (Intimidating for him, to be clear. I think it's kind of fun.)

Me: Is it? I mean, it could be if you decide to see it that way. You could view me as a woman who has built her world so much that I don't need a man for anything. Or, you could choose to get excited about everything I've accomplished! Think of what I could bring into your world!

There's more silence as the dude continues to be intimidated.

Me: You can be intimidated, but that's your choice. Listen, I hate to cut this short, but I'm at my next appointment. I'll send you a couple of podcasts to listen to that may give you some clarity on me.

Dude: Ok, that is another way to look at it. I'll give them a listen. Have a great day!

I sent the dude my PowerWomen podcast episode about dating standards, and I never heard from him again. So much for standards leading to instant catnip status!

I won't lie to you: it can be disappointing when we uphold our standards and find ourselves getting shut down. But let me tell you this: women like you and me are to be celebrated, and anyone who is intimidated by us is not the right fit. If he's not up to the challenge, he's not a man of quality. With the trifecta of beauty, brains, and success, we often aren't single for long (unless it's by choice), and if we are, it's likely because we've failed to define one of two things:

1. Our own worth
2. What exactly we're looking for in a partner

As soon as we discern these two pieces (in this order), we can learn to identify when a potential partner brings equal or higher value to the table, and we can find men who meet our standards. That's why I've used the diamond motif throughout this book. It's not about getting the ring; it's about strength and worth—our own and what we seek to find in others.

When I was in a difficult marriage and heading into a divorce, my father gave me some of the best advice: "Darlin'," he said, "if you trade in one model with one set of problems, you're just going to get another model with a different set of problems. So, you might as well deal with the set you got." These words seemed so cynical at first. Why would I stay in an unhappy marriage for fear of not finding anything better? I may have been too damn naïve, but I thought dating would be easy. As a budding PowerWoman, I was a catch, right?

Of course, when I started dating, my daddy's words became crystal clear. I hadn't been out there since high school, and my marriage hadn't taught me much about my own value or what I wanted in a partner. I quickly learned just how difficult dating can be, and I realized if I went into the search for a new partner with the same expectations and assumptions I'd brought into my marriage, I was going to wind up in similarly mismatched relationships over and over and over. My daddy was right: simply trading one for another wasn't going to do me any good. There was no way settling for my marriage was the right choice—for myself, my husband, or our children—so he wasn't entirely on point. But if I wanted to attract a newer, better model of a partner, I had to work on myself first. I had to learn my value, set my standards, and define exactly what I wanted a relationship to look like.

But how do we determine our value? How do we know what kind of partner will meet our standards? And, more importantly, are we ready for him when he shows up at our door? That's the real struggle—preparing ourselves to attract the partners we want by building our own strength and confidence. When you bring that kind of power to your dating life—when you're clear about what you value in others, what your personal standards are, and what you want in your relationships—you'll find what you're looking for a lot faster. And that's the challenge I hope this book will help you overcome.

My singlehood journey wasn't like anyone else's I'd seen, and it still isn't. That's a good thing. The journey looks different for each of us. But that doesn't mean we need to go it alone. Over the last five years, I've talked with at least three hundred women—women in their twenties and women in their sixties—about their romantic lives. Listening to stories about their dating journeys—which have been so different from each other's and from mine—has taught me that, though every experience is different, there is one common denominator: we are all continually learning about ourselves and refining our dating standards. As I've talked with these women and lived out my own experiences, I started asking myself the same questions over and over again: What would I tell my twenty-five-year-old self now? What if I could have used what I now know to empower myself back then? How can the lessons I've learned help other women—at every age and in every stage of the Singlehood journey—understand just how valuable they are and just how powerful they can be?

My stories look nothing like *Sex and the City*. My experiences in the Singlehood have been everything short of glamorous. Like many of you, I've had to fail miserably in the dating space in order to discover my worth, my confidence, and what I want in a partner. But even as it started to feel like Lizzo's "Truth Hurts" was becoming my anthem—like I was never going to find a man I didn't need to wash out of my hair, much less a great man.

Every failed date and every discouraging moment were learning opportunities, and what I finally gleaned from those moments was a series of pillars, for myself and for my relationships, that have helped me measure my worth and define my standards. These pillars are simply areas in my life where I've worked to define who I am and what I want, and I want to share them with you so that you can build your own pillars. In this book, I'm offering you a guide to discovering your authentic self, your self-worth, and your standards for dating—and to honoring those in every new adventure you take in the Singlehood. I'm offering clarity and empowerment to help you find confidence, fun, and a dating life that is fulfilling and productive. And I'm offering it here so that, hopefully, you can avoid learning some of these lessons in the difficult (and sometimes utterly ridiculous) ways I've had to learn them.

CLARITY IS POWER

Maybe it's because I'm from the South, or maybe it's because I'm single, but I hear the phrase, "There are plenty of fish in the sea!" constantly. So many people I encounter think I need comforting because I'm in the Singlehood, and this is their go-to encouragement. But let me tell you something: I don't think these people really understand fishing. I, on the other hand, grew up fishing with my papa and my paw paw, and my mother has become quiet the fly fisherwoman in her later years. Based on all of this experience, I've made a few observations: First, fishing takes a lot of practice. Second, it requires you to be quiet and patient. Third, you end up having to throw back a lot of nasty fish before you catch one you can filet, bread, fry, and eat! It is *not* a simple or quick process! I mean, do you know how big the ocean is? This sea of men we're fishing in is vast, deep, and full of variety, and there are more fish to choose from now than ever before. In fact, *The Observer* reported recently that, while 72% of Americans were married in 1970, a full 45% of the population was single in 2018.[1] How many of those fish am I going to have to cut loose before I find one worth reeling in?

Once upon a time, the dating pool was limited mainly to your

6

immediate area, and dating entailed old-fashioned courtship practices like writing letters to your loved one and taking walks together with a chaperone not far behind. Back then, matches were made for love, but they were also made for social and economic status. Today, the pond has grown into an ocean. We're no longer limited by geography, and we can meet potential partners online or on countless dating apps as well as in real life. Economics are no longer the primary factor in determining a relationship's worth, though they're still certainly on the table. And the risks of dating have grown in many ways as the pool has expanded: along with the old-fashioned heartbreak, assaults, and general shitty behavior that unfortunately still exist today, there are also reports of new, Internet-enabled offenses such a fraud, theft, and more. Unlike fishing, dating is not a hobby. Dating is a serious commitment (not necessarily to an individual partner but to the process, at the very least), and it can have serious ramifications on our lives.

Many people still date seriously with the long term in mind, while others take a much more casual approach. And for some, those varied expectations are the biggest stressor in the dating game. When we enter anything with unclear or unrealistic expectations, we set ourselves up for disappointment. Many of us expect to find fun, excitement, courtship, and ultimately love in today's dating landscape. Unfortunately, many of us are likewise disappointed. Funny man and magician Phil Pivnick puts it like this: "Online dating is like online shopping—except that with online shopping, you're looking for things people really like, and you get them cheap. If you're online dating, you're looking for people no one wants, and it's $50 a month." Preach, brother! Someone pass the offering plate!

So, with so many fish and no great way to vet them before you hook them, today's dating sea is, at first glance, a scary place. But it doesn't have to be. What you have to discern is what, exactly, you're fishing for. If you don't know your standards, how do you know when to reel someone in rather than toss him back? One thing is for sure: if you don't like what you're catching, cast your net to another side of the boat, because you never have to settle. A former coach rocked my world with these simple words of wisdom: "Claire, you get to choose." Never forget that. We get to choose who we want to be and how we want to show up. We also choose how we spend our time and who we spend it with. This book will help you determine how to make those choices.

(Now, I recognize that, as we throw back one fish after another, it can be easy to get discouraged. So as we learn to uphold our standards and make confident choices, it's important to learn how to find the silver lining—even in the bad dates. Here's one of my favorites: my grocery bill. I met with my financial advisor recently and, as we went over my budget, she said, "How is your grocery bill so low?" You know why? Because of dating. Every date I go on is fewer groceries I have to buy. Don't get me wrong: I'm happy to pay for my own meal, and I often do, but the less time I spend in the grocery store, the better, in my book! Obviously, in order for a man to last in my life, he has to prove he's worth more than groceries—just like we women have to be worth more than arm candy—but if the date is just mediocre and the groceries are good, then there's my silver lining! Thanks for the groceries, and best of luck in your journey.)

When a potential relationship is a nonstarter, another silver lining is the opportunity to learn more about ourselves and our standards. Recently, a wonderful man I had gone on only a couple of dates with called me to talk business. Though the dating hadn't stuck, we had become friends and business associates. Never burn a bridge. He mentioned a newly single man in our market he thought I should try to date. (You know you are a real single girl when your former dates try to set you up with other men.) As usual, I was extremely curious. But before I could accept the setup, and since we were on the subject of romance, I had some questions to ask my former-fling-turned-business-associate. In business, when I fail to obtain a client or meet a goal, I always ask how I can improve. Here was my opportunity to do the same in my dating life. So I asked him, "What was it? What held you back?" He let me know I had set the bar too high with my dating pillars. Oh, it was such clarity! It wasn't something I had failed to bring to the table. The problem was that he didn't value himself enough to meet my standards, nor was he willing to try. And yet, although he preferred to settle, he understood my standards and recognized my value enough to set me up with someone else. What if I hadn't had those standards? What if I hadn't been clear about them with this man, or what if I had decided not to hold to them in this scenario? Eventually, our misaligned expectations would have resulted in one of us becoming heartbroken again. Clarity is so powerful. Don't be afraid to discover your standards; they will become your guide in the Singlehood, and they'll save you from wasting your time with the wrong partners.

Can your standards ever be too high, as this man suggested? Absolutely not! They are yours, and only you can determine what is right for your world. For evidence that your standards matter, just look at Amy Webb. She is a futurist who gave an amazing TED Talk on the data points of her dating journey.[2] She created her standards and then created an elaborate scoring system to evaluate potential partners. Ultimately, Webb had seventy-two data points that defined the standards her ideal man would meet. Lo and behold, she met a man who *surpassed* those standards. I'm not suggesting we each need seventy-two hurdles or standards, but Amy Webb never settled and neither should we!

Having clarity about our standards allows us to choose who earns our time and who gets thrown back into the dating pool. My papa used to say, "Everybody has standards; some people's are just low." Set your standards, set them high, and stay firm in them, because the old saying rings truer now than ever before: there *are* plenty of fish in the sea!

THE MIRROR AND THE LENS: WHY WE NEED SELF PILLARS AND DATING PILLARS

I've had conversations with many people about the dynamics of men and women in personal and professional relationships, I've heard a wide range of opinions, and I've learned we each make up our own stories about ourselves and about relationships as we form our opinions and standards. Often, these stories are built to place the blame for our dating struggles on circumstance, on other people—anywhere but on ourselves. And I was guilty of that, too, for a long time. What I finally learned is that, when we each take responsibility for our own actions and behaviors and consciously reflect on the patterns we're seeing in our lives, that's when change will start to occur. What I mean to say is that forming your pillars and setting your standards will require you to grow personally. It won't be easy, but when you begin to see your personal growth as you look in the mirror, then you will be able to establish effective pillars in the dating space. But we have to get ourselves right before we can get our relationships right, and that's why we must establish our "self pillars" prior to forming our dating pillars. We must be confident in who we are in order to attract a partner whose standards align with ours. The more you look in the mirror and reflect on yourself, the clearer your lens will become in the dating space.

While I was starting my dating journey, I was also transitioning into single parenthood and sharing custody with my ex-husband. Many days I wanted to wallow in my grief over my marriage or my deep sadness in being apart from my children for half of every week, and many days I did. But I knew I couldn't stay there if I wanted to build a new and better life for myself. We all have these kinds of breakdowns in our relationships and in life. But they present opportunities to grow, to make breakthroughs, to change our patterns, and to decide who we are and who we want to grow into.

I had a small local village of close friends, but I needed more. I was recovering from a heartbreak that caused a breakdown, and I was ready to move on to some breakthroughs. So, I launched social media groups for PowerWomen. In less than a year, we had more than 6,000 members. At the time, I was also working with coaches to help me build my business. These people were big thinkers, driven, and innovative, and they genuinely cared about my success in all areas of my life. They became my partners in many ways, offering support that I no longer had through a romantic relationship. The people I surrounded myself with pushed me and made me better in all areas of life. I was making more money than I had dreamed possible, I was being offered leadership opportunities, and my kids were soaring. I was a PowerWoman and a PowerMom on the rise.

All of that support, growth, and success was important, but it didn't stop me from failing miserably in the dating world, and sometimes those failures threatened to eclipse every positive experience in other areas of my life. But rather than let them block out all the light, I learned how to use them as an impetus to pause, reflect, seek the counsel of my village and mentors, and realize I had some work to do—on myself, my outlook, and my approach to dating. From that work—from looking in the mirror and from refining my dating lens—emerged the pillars in this book.

A mirror can be a woman's worst enemy. We tend to pick ourselves apart when we look at ourselves, so it's often much easier just to avoid it. But I decided it was time to look carefully in that mirror at all aspects of my life. When I was presented with obstacles and disappointments, the mirror reflected them as opportunities to grow myself rather than find fault with others. It was often difficult to look in the mirror, but it provided much-needed perspective every time. When men were texting me late at night, I decided to look in the mirror. When dating apps turned up nothing but disappointment, I decided to look in the mirror. When I found myself in Europe with a man who had brought me there only to ask me for money (yes, really—but more on that later), I decided to look in the mirror.

In this life journey, the people around us also act as mirrors in a way, in that we find in others what we find in ourselves. The more you grow in any given area, the more you will attract others who are like-minded. If you desire a partner who lives up to your standards for each pillar, then you must define and meet those standards for yourself first. Then, he will surface in your life. You have to keep looking in the mirror. It may be difficult at first, but it will get easier! (After all, look at you, gorgeous! How could you not stop and stare?) As you work with your mirror to build your self pillars, you gain inner strength, a true sense of your own worth, and the confidence to clarify your dating pillars. Our dating prospects will see our value and our worth based on how we treat ourselves, and caring for ourselves only comes from knowing and loving ourselves. In other words, girl, you gotta know and love all of you before you can attract the right man! The self pillars are all about asking yourself these questions:

Do I show myself love like I do others?
How do I want a man to care for me, and how am I already
doing that for myself?
Do I hold myself to the same standards I expect from others?

(Go ahead, ask yourself. Think about your answers. If you feel inspired, try some journaling. I'll wait.)

As I learned difficult lessons over and over again, I learned how to answer these questions in a way that made me proud, and I discovered my pillars for dating as a PowerWoman. I have learned that when a person comes into my world, there are a few more questions I need to ask myself—especially if he is a man and I want to start to figure out whether he has the potential to meet my standards: 1) Why is this person coming into my world? 2) What are they here to teach me? 3) How can I help them?

I didn't always ask myself these questions, but using them to reflect on the people who have come across my path has been so enlightening.

My dad was right—sort of. Nobody is perfect, but that doesn't mean you can't find somebody who is nearly perfect *for you*. That's what the dating pillars are all about. They're a guide to help you discern what your dating standards look like. My coach was right too: "You Choose!" You choose the standards that hold up each pillar, and you choose what is most important in your dating journey. These all look very different to each of us. What's important is that we are clear in our expectations so we can determine whether we truly align with a potential partner.

HOW THIS BOOK CAN HELP

Defining these pillars has determined how I live my life and who shows up in my dating world, and the same can be true for you. Throughout this book, I share the essential pillars for self and for dating—five of each. Each pillar is an area we *all* need to work on, but the specific standards you set for each pillar are your own. After all, we all have different experiences and values, so while there may be some overlap, it would be counterproductive to try to force my specific standards into anyone else's life. I will tell stories and write about defining my standards, but my standards are not yours. I don't know what your standards are—only you can know that—but I do know that you need to define standards in each of these areas to feel confident, joyful, and excited about the people you're inviting into your life.

The other piece of the puzzle is that the pillars may not be equally important, and their importance may vary from one PowerWoman to another. Depending on your story, your journey, your beliefs, your sense of worth, and so much more, some pillars will be more meaningful to you than others. For example, the money pillar: I've worked hard to build a very successful business that allows me to live the life I want, send my kids to private school, travel, and more, all on my own. So for me, finding a partner who is financially independent is highly important. That pillar may be less important to you for any number of reasons, but it's still important to get clear on your beliefs and values around money so you can ensure you align with your partner. (Let's remember, money issues are a primary cause of divorce.)

Throughout the book, I've presented questions to help you reflect on your patterns and define your standards. Take the time to really think about them, journal about them, and come up with honest answers. It's the only way to get to the growth and clarity you want and deserve.

I have also created special content throughout the book for those of you who are single moms like me, and I've even included a pillar just for you. For single moms, the perspective on the growth and dating issues in this book can be a bit different. As a single mom, I'm always aware that I'm the model for my children, and that includes how I approach dating. It's my job to prioritize and protect them.

As you read, please keep in mind that while I hold many titles, licensed therapist (or anything in the mental health field, for that matter) is not one of them. I am that girlfriend who will speak fierce truth to you and pose tough questions in order to help you seek joy in your life, just as others have done for me. Looking in the mirror is not easy, and many times I've needed a third-party therapist or coach to show me the mirror to overcome hurdles in my personal and professional growth. Without these guides in my world, I hate to think of where I would be, and I encourage everyone to seek a third-party professional to lean on when you need it.

In order to recognize my value and establish my pillars, I had to fail often and fail miserably. In writing this book, it's my hope that you learn from my mistakes so we can rise together!

AUTHOR'S NOTE

Throughout this book, some details and names have been changed or omitted to protect the guilty.

ONE

Does History Repeat Itself?

I'm not sure how much my accent is coming through, but I'm Southern. Like my compatriots, I love God, fried food, and gentlemen. The Arkansas town where I was raised had about eighteen thousand people, and it was a perfect depiction of a somewhat modern Mayberry—at least, to my youthful eyes. When I was in high school, the gas station was still full-service, and you could run charge accounts at the local pharmacy, dry cleaners, and department store. Friday night football games were a city-wide event—and they still are!

All through high school, I dated a sweet Mormon boy while leading what appeared to be a pretty idyllic high school life—cheerleader, student council, friends galore. I was a "good girl." My father had put the fear of the Almighty God into me growing up, and it helped that he was an influential attorney in town. The thought of coming home in the back of a police cruiser...well, I was fairly certain my fate would be death by lecture, followed by boarding school!

Mom was a stay-at-home mother and went to all the Bible study fellowships available, always with a casserole in hand. Papa was head of the Democratic Party in our county and a deacon in our church. We were the ideal family for the next church billboard on the interstate—at least, until their divorce!

At seventeen, I met my future ex-husband. At twenty, I married him like a good Southern girl. I was inexperienced and naïve. I was so young I couldn't even drink at my own damn wedding! Let me be clear: I do not recommend this timeline. Every young woman should take her time and enjoy her twenties—really enjoy them. This is our time to discover our future potential, to start building our careers, and to develop enough experience to discern whether a dude has half a brain in his head or any sort of future potential. In a perfect world, our twenties are when we define our pillars—and train men to live up to them.

If you're reading this after your twenties, don't be discouraged! I waited until my thirties to learn these lessons, and I've met many fabulous, confident, amazing women who waited even longer. After my divorce, reliving my twenties was no longer an option, since my children were watching my model. Realizing that I wasn't twenty-five anymore was difficult at times, but I started to become clear on the woman I wanted to be, and I continued to ask myself the question, "What do you need to do in order to become that woman?" Making hard pivots in my actions and mindset and shedding the patterns of my past was a difficult journey, but I had to do those things in order to learn how to date in a healthy way with my children by my side. The point is, no matter how old you are, it's not too late, I promise. But, girlfriend, what are you waiting for?

What came before, during, and after my marriage had an awful lot to do with the way I was raised and the relationship and dating patterns my parents and the rest of my family had taught me. Before and during my marriage, I was fighting against those patterns, and afterward, I fell right into them. You'll understand why soon enough.

Once we gain clarity on the positive and negative patterns in our lives, it becomes easier to make healthier choices and have a more productive dating life. If we don't gain clarity on our past, then how do we know how to get what we want in our future? If we don't recognize our patterns and learn from our mistakes, then how will we keep from repeating them? If we don't stop repeating the patterns, then what are we imposing on our children? Do you want to break the chain of patterns in your family, and how do you intend to make that happen?

Have you reflected on your past, the values you were raised with, and how those things have shaped you and your dating life?
Do you want to repeat your parents' patterns?
What people and events have influenced your decisions or perspectives, and do you need to change them moving forward?
How are you choosing to change negative patterns in order to make healthier decisions and empower yourself?

LESSONS OF A SINGLE MOM

As a mother in the Singlehood, I no longer had a spouse to help me hold myself accountable and to watch the patterns I was modeling for my children. Everything now rested on my shoulders—everything. What new habits was I going to engage in, and who was I going to allow into my world? Was I going to go into a depression and allow my children to witness despair and unhealthy coping mechanisms? Was I going to introduce them to everyone I went out with? The goal of attracting a spouse seemed frivolous when I stopped to think about the impact I was having on my children during my singlehood. Where was my focus? I realized that my patterns had huge implications on my children and their futures, and that had a powerful impact on the way I approached dating.

BOY, BYE

I've already told you I was the "good girl" growing up. But when I tell you I lived a sheltered life, I'm not exaggerating. I never drank as a kid and hardly ever as a young adult. I had never even *seen* drugs, including marijuana, until I was 35-years-old and divorced. But I had been exposed to my parents' wild and crazy marriage and subsequent dating lives, and that created a fascinating dating model for me. My parents divorced when I was 10-years-old, and everything about that "perfect family" persona we had went to hell! Their individual responses to their divorce were polar opposites. Let's start with dear ol' Dad.

I have always had a close and complex relationship with my father. However, dating is not his strong suit. After my parents divorced, he dated every single woman in the county! Praise sweet baby Jesus in the manger for not giving him access to dating apps; he did well enough without them. My papa is charming, worldly, fun as hell, not bad looking, brilliant, and successful. He also possesses a "shock and awe" factor. It starts with the way he dresses. He is famous for his white suits. (If that doesn't scream "Southern attorney," I don't know what does!) I don't even know how many he owns. There are suits with long coats and short coats and suits in off white, ecru, and stark white. And each one has a vest and matching dress shoes. "Dapper" doesn't do him justice. Finding a date? Are you kidding me? He was one of the hottest tickets in town.

People were setting him up right and left. And because he is one of the horniest men to walk this earth, he had a different date every day of the week. I had the fortune—or misfortune—of meeting most of them. After they left, I would get my dad's commentary on them.

Papa had a reputation for going through women quickly, but he also remarried quickly. He met a woman, and they were married within three months. I now have a fantastic brother from that union, but it only lasted nine years. It was a tumultuous marriage that taught me many lessons. Let's just say that during my freshman year of college we were ready for *The Jerry Springer Show*!

Papa is a man with a huge heart, and he loves nothing more than to help others. So, when a project woman comes along, and when she is also young and beautiful, Papa can't help himself. For example, while he was married to his second wife, he fell for the convict. She was currently on parole in three different states. The most recent conviction? Attempted murder of her ex-boyfriend with a deadly weapon. Her current place of employment was a gentleman's strip club outside of town. During her courtship with my father, she and her 14-year-old son lived down the street from us in a rented house. Papa bought her the same living room furniture we had at our house, the same china pattern my grandmother had given me, the same crystal he and his second wife had, and a white Sebring convertible. Again, Jerry Springer was just waiting for us to call.

The only time I ever saw this woman was when she violated parole and got sent straight to the county jail. I made a visit. Everyone who read the local paper knew exactly what her relationship was with my father, and I had to see this situation with my own eyes. I had worked at the county courthouse in high school, and I'd made a lot of friends. So I walked into the county jail, waved to the jailor, and went straight to the sheriff, a divorced woman with strong principles. She and I had a fabulous relationship, and she could see my emotions pouring out of my eyes and my whole body. I was shaking with anger and shame. Legally and professionally, there was no way the sheriff could let me have contact with the convict. They weren't married (yet), and Papa hadn't adopted her even though the age difference would have allowed for it, so I wasn't considered family. But sister sheriff knew I needed to lay eyes on this woman, so she brought the convict to the window and let me watch while they went over her legal options again. She was blond, thin, and beautiful, even in orange. She had some mad male attraction skills, bless her heart.

After her arrest, she headed back to the penitentiary in Kentucky, which caused a break in the courtship. (Long distance is rough enough without the added complication of a jail cell, right ladies?) So, back into the dating pool my father went. This time it was wild! Really wild! Of course, I was also older, more in the know, and paying closer attention. The women rolled in and out of my father's house and his life, and it seemed the number-one criteria was that prospects be at least fifteen years his junior.

His only boundary was that if the women were younger than me, they were off limits. He called it "The Claire Rule." Literally.

Otherwise, they were fair game. There was the woman who lived in a teepee in her backyard. Yes, she was Native American, and I really did like her, but when I met her all I wanted to ask about was indoor plumbing. There was the woman I referred to as "the skunk" because of the white streak down the middle of her black hair. She was one of the most beautiful women I've ever met in person, completely stunning, but she had a backwoods Southern accent that was so strong even I couldn't understand half of what she said. She was a hairdresser, and my dad just happened to help her finance the renovation of her entire salon. I think she felt she had to hang around for a while after that. I never learned to understand her, and eventually she broke my papa's heart.

I had thought that relationship was Papa's rock bottom, but he still hadn't found the basement. So, when Papa got the convict out of prison in Kentucky and brought her back home to live with him, what could we say? He wanted this woman. He went to great lengths to be with this woman. The lesson? If a man really wants you, he'll come and get you. Hell, he'll even come and get you out of prison.

Even though she came to live with Papa and he tried to introduce us, I never met the convict. He desperately wanted for us to all be the postcard for the prison system, but I had recently gotten married at the ripe age of twenty, and this *Pretty Woman* dream just didn't play out in our heads the same way. They lived together for five months before the wedding day. It was a Thanksgiving wedding, and I heard it was lovely. I chose not to attend. Their union was short and tumultuous, and after three months of wedded bliss, they divorced.

Many of us face a roadblock in our journey that causes us to take a step back and change our patterns. An alcoholic gets a DWI and starts attending AA. Somebody goes bankrupt and finally seeks real financial help. The split with the convict was my father's roadblock, and he has shifted his behavior since their divorce. He hasn't even dated much at all in the past fifteen years.

So, how did all of this affect me? Well, first let's address the assumption that I was at a higher risk to become a divorcée because I came from a home of divorced parents. But *Business Insider* published studies showing that this assumption is false. The real concerning patterns of our past are the levels of family conflict (divorce or no) and the way that conflict is handled.[3] Many times a divorce will eliminate the conflict and allow for peace and healing, preventing the children from repeating their parents' patterns in the future. But, as you've seen, the aftermath of my parents' divorce wasn't exactly peaceful, and I found myself falling right into their patterns.

It wasn't until I had my heart broken that I started to understand what my father might have been going through all those years. Fortunately, my journey hadn't involved any convicts (or convictions of my own, for that matter), but the instability of meeting all my father's girlfriends growing up meant I gave myself permission to date—a lot and without much discernment. After all, the women my father introduced me to had not established their own inner pillars (or if they had, they were not pillars I wanted to model) so I hadn't learned to establish mine. Through my father's womanizing, I became a man-eater.

Eventually, I realized I had lost my mind in the Singlehood as well. I had been trying to ignore the discomfort and the pain of the past. I held a title I had fought very hard never to have: divorcée. I'd inherited enough pain from so much divorce in my family that I had fought hard against imposing the same on my children at any level. But now I know that, no matter how hard we may try, we cannot control others' words and actions, and sometimes trying to hold onto a bad marriage or an unrealistic dream holds us back more than we realize. I decided if I was unable to make my marriage work, I was going to make my divorce work. My ex-husband and I committed to allowing for a peaceful divorce and eliminating the conflict in our home, hopefully preventing future conflicts for our children. Now more than ever, there was a need to make sure I was creating the best environment for my children, because my actions were shaping their future.

There are countless studies about how women are impacted by their relationships with their fathers, and how that shows up in our communication, relationships, and choices in business. One particularly fascinating tidbit I've learned was that, according to the Institute for Family Studies, a woman's relationship with her father is more impactful than her relationship with her mother.[4] Darlin', I'm no psychologist or expert in this field, but I know I would be a good case study. The commonality in all my reading was this: women who had close relationships with their fathers in childhood typically had better communication skills, a stronger sense of their own value, and a better ability to deal with stress. They also tended to model masculine behavior and career choices as a result of their fathers' mentorship. As you would imagine, women who did not have strong relationships with their fathers when they were young fell into superficial or strictly physical relationships and lacked direction in their careers. There are many exceptions, of course, but the general findings followed these patterns. I recognized myself in all of them.

What had my patterns been since my divorce? The mirror was not kind to me here! Most relationships—including every single person I met online or from an app—didn't get past a coffee date. That was my version of a one-night stand. If a dude got past the first date, I usually hung on to him for an average of four weeks. I'd met every one of those men organically—not online. When I recognized this pattern, I immediately got off all dating technology while I evaluated what was working and what wasn't.

One thing was clear: my post-divorce life was beginning to parallel my father's, and I needed to make a pivot fast. I wasn't willing to repeat his journey. I had lowered my standards, and I was saying yes to too many of the wrong type of men. It was time to pivot and say no to these men in order to say yes to the pillars in my life.

What have been your patterns in
your previous relationships?
What are your parents' or mentors' relationship patterns,
and how are you repeating them?
What patterns do you want to model, and
how are you making that happen?
What do you need to let go of in order to
create healthier patterns?

DECADES OF DATING

Mom was a hot mess after the divorce. This break in her life brought a grief that I had never seen before, and while my dad jumped right back into the dating game, it took Mom two decades of dating one man to get back in.

Remember, this was back in the stone ages, when there were landlines and no Internet. So, the only dates Mom went on were with people her friends set her up with. Like most of us, she was guarded, and when she encountered anyone similar to my papa, she ran. Shortly after the divorce, a friend set Mom up with a man whom she really liked, and they dated for eighteen years. I know, your mouth just dropped. Yes, they *dated* for eighteen years, but they never married. Mom was settling, and on some level, she saw it. That's why she didn't marry him. But she didn't see her own potential yet, either. She was learning who she was and what she wanted. This man adored her, but they didn't match. Finally, Mom recognized that, and they mutually agreed to go their separate ways.

I should note that, though dating someone for eighteen years may be unusual in general, it wasn't that out of the ordinary in my family. My grandmother had dated a man for fifty-four years without marrying him. My aunt, my mother's sister, once dated a man for more than ten years. The women in my family are amazing and very successful, but when it comes to dating, there is a very distinct pattern.

Anyway, after several years of getting to know herself, my mother finally did get back into the game, and she played it well! Specifically, Mom discovered online dating. My now-ex-husband and I were comfortably married at that point, and we were parents by then, so bath time was often the biggest event of the night. One day Mom called to ask if she could "come over to see the kids." Note that my mother lived thirty miles away from my house in a suburb of the city, and she didn't come over daily. But she came over that afternoon, and everyone chitchatted as normal. Then, I noticed she'd brought a toiletry bag filled with makeup and a curling iron. When I asked her about it, she brushed it off, saying she had a dinner close by and thought she'd get ready at our house. Like I'd done many times in my childhood, I followed Mom to the bathroom to keep up our conversation while she did her hair and makeup.

Since I'd grown up and moved out of the house, we hadn't spent nearly so much time chatting in the bathroom and especially not in my house. But she repeated this abnormal song and dance in our guest bath three nights in a row, never willing to linger on what she was up to. When had my mother's social life become so active? On the third night, I met her at the garage door and demanded, "What the hell is going on?" To this day, I have never seen my mother look as ecstatic as she did in that moment. She looked like she'd simultaneously struck gold and discovered the Fountain of Youth. Her giddiness was contagious, but still, I was not prepared for what she did next: Mom tugged me into my own kitchen, whipped out her laptop computer, and introduced me to online dating.

It had happened: my mother had become the hottest thing on the market, and she had put it all online! She was beautiful, educated, financially independent, the mother of two grown, independent children, and smart as hell. Her biggest problem now was how to manage all the men. So, like every smart woman, she had created a spreadsheet. We looked at all their profiles, compared and contrasted them, and charted them according to what was important to her. All of the men on the spreadsheet got nicknames. It helped keep them all straight, and it's a habit I've adopted, myself. (I give every boy a nickname if he makes it past the first date. I know for a fact that men do this too.)

As an aside, Mom's side of the family is Cajun, and we all love some good Cajun food. Unfortunately, there is only one good Cajun restaurant in our area, and—you guessed it—it's near my house. Since Mom called the shots, she had lined up dinner dates with a different man at the same Cajun restaurant every night that week. She was ready to try everything on the menu!

Eventually, Mom found a man who was younger than she was, and of course he melted her butter! This guy was very nice looking, but he had no real job, no real stable home situation, and three teenage daughters. Oh, and he was only ten years older than me. Mom was discovering her beauty, her value, and her body, but in doing so, she was acting like she was 16 again.

For example, soon after she began her online dating adventures, Mom had to have an outpatient procedure at one of the local hospitals. The night before the procedure, she broke it off with another dude from the spreadsheet so he wouldn't show up. She only wanted the young buck there to hold her hand. During the procedure, the young buck and I went to the cafeteria to get a snack, and when I saw a colleague of Mom's, she asked if he was *my* husband! Jesus, take the wheel! Before the procedure, things got really turned around. As the medical team came in to ask her questions and make sure she was alert, their eyes widened. Mom and her young buck were making out in the bed while she was hooked up to an IV pole with tubes flying everywhere. To a person, the medical crew started to leave the room until they realized I was there, ready to be the adult. If I couldn't answer the questions they asked, I would hit Mom's foot and yell at her to come up for air. Bless the anesthesiologist. I just told him to go ahead and knock her out, and I also requested something for my own nausea.

When a woman finds herself in the Singlehood, it is not uncommon for her to want to "fix it." I imagine that's what my mother was going through during her eighteen-year romance and subsequent flings. This new situation we're thrown into is so uncomfortable that we want to "fix it" as soon as possible. We're desperate to go back to the normalcy we once knew. This feeling causes people to date the wrong people, remarry too quickly, or spend eighteen years in ill-suited relationships. My mother was no exception, and neither was I. I thought I could "fix" my situation by finding a partner in order to make my life to go back to normal again. I was so afraid of repeating the pattern the women in my family had established—divorce followed by decades-long, commitment-free relationships—that I swung the opposite direction, following both my parents' footsteps into a series of flings. The last thing I wanted to do was repeat either of my parents' patterns, but there I was.

When I entered the Singlehood, PowerWomen came out of the woodwork with dating advice for me. The common phrase was "Whatever you do, do not settle!" Settling seemed to be something many women regretted, and they wanted to pass their wisdom along to me so I could avoid repeating their mistakes. But settling didn't seem to be my problem. I was working so hard *not* to settle that I was being too guarded, and that kept PowerMen at a distance.

At this point, I was still dating men at the rate my father had dated women, but in my efforts to avoid falling into that dating-for-decades pattern, I built walls that were keeping fantastic men out of boyfriend territory. I was not allowing myself to be vulnerable and open-minded. Instead, my defense mechanism was to eliminate suitors almost immediately, sometimes without meeting them. Keeping a man at a distance seemed safe, but the combination of my mother's and father's patterns had landed me where I least wanted to be: alone. It was time to stop repeating the patterns of my past and allow my heart to soften in order for the walls to come down.

What are the patterns in your family?
How are the patterns in your family showing up
in your world?
Are you happy with that?
If not, how do you plan to change them?

MY POWERWOMAN PATTERNS

Was having a mediocre dinner partner better than having no one at all? Did I even want someone around all the time? What did I want a relationship to look like? I had to learn so many lessons about my family and myself to realize what strong women I had actually come from. I had feared falling into their patterns, but I discovered that they were women with standards, who were financially independent and remained single by choice, despite multiple opportunities to marry. For example, both of my grand-mothers are in their 90s and live at home alone.

My maternal grandmother became a single mother in the six-ties, when women did not get divorced. After her divorce, she earned her master's degree, raised three girls, managed rental property, paid for three sets of private school and college tuition as well as three weddings, developed a subdivision and built a house in her seventies, and retired in her 80s. In the meantime, she took care of her mother and father into their 80s and 100s. She is a PowerWoman.

Mom is a PowerWoman too—much more than I ever realized

when I was growing up. She went back to school for a second degree, becoming a nurse practitioner at age 38, and she is excellent at what she does. I realized my mother was raised with a no-limits mindset, and she was able to empower herself by starting a new career, designing her own life, and becoming financially independent.

These were patterns I *wanted* to emulate.

It wasn't only my family's patterns that influenced me either; there were plenty of PowerWomen bringing their own patterns into my life and not only in the dating space.

According to the National Association of Realtors, 67% of realtors are women.[5] I entered the real estate industry at an early age, and I was suddenly surrounded by PowerWomen. I was blessed to have mentorship at my fingertips. Seeing women succeed in my field at an international level, I gave myself permission to follow suit. Having women in the office to turn to has been priceless.

Women cringe at the thought of "becoming their mothers," but in reading and studying how women throughout history have chosen to rise and achieve success, I've realized something: each of these women has chosen to heal the wounds of her past and carry on the positive patterns she's learned from the women in her lives. We should learn from our mothers—both literal and metaphorical—but we can also strive to become them in many ways, embracing their strength, confidence, and power for ourselves. In an interview with NPR, Maya Angelou discussed her rather erratic childhood.[6] She was raised in many different homes with many different family members, but despite the negative impacts this could have had, Angelou chose to embrace the good, heal, and focus on love without limits, and that's evident in her legacy. "I'm Maya Angelou—whatever that means to whomever it means—because my mother loved me, and my grandmother loved me, and my brother loved me," she says. "And they all told me I could do whatever I wanted to do."

I had been limiting myself in many ways, but it was time to show my children there were no limits to love and achievement. I started taking my responsibility seriously to reflect on the legacy I was creating for and leaving with my children. I focused entirely on living with purpose, pouring out love to others, and adapting that no-limits mindset my mother had inherited from her mother. Fear took a backseat to everything else when I realized that I could have excuses or I could have results, but I could not have both. It was time to make my choice.

*What patterns have the PowerWomen in your life
brought into your world?
Which of those patterns do you want to hold onto?
Which would you rather let go of?
What is your legacy, and how are your
choices building that?
How are you limiting yourself, your opportunities,
and others?
What excuses are you telling yourself in order to
avoid going after your goals?
What is your greatest fear, and what are you doing
to overcome it?*

TWO

The Emotions and Emojis

I love to ride my bike by the river along the trails near my house. It's my release. One day, I bumped into a male friend who was out running with another man. We chatted for a minute and went our separate ways. The next day, the other man reached out to me through my real estate website. He had Googled me, found me, and followed up! It was a great first impression, even though I wasn't connecting the dots yet. When I called thinking he needed a realtor, he set me straight real quick by asking me to lunch.

He was nice and good-looking, but he was fourteen years older, and that didn't sit right with me. Remember my papa's patterns? One of the guidelines I had cultivated for myself as a response was to date men pretty close to my own age. But it was working between us, so when he asked me to go out of town with him one weekend, I said yes. After the getaway, the age issue kept coming up for me, and it manifested itself primarily in his communication style: he texted me all day every day about everything—with emojis. I couldn't bring myself to mirror the behavior—constant texting just isn't my style, and while I appreciate a well-placed emoji as much as the next person, the incessant use felt immature—so I knew it was time to cut it off. If there is ever a time you feel one communicates on the same level of your teenager and he is in his 50s, that should give you pause.

I asked him to meet me at Starbucks. I made it a point to arrive early and get my own coffee. When he joined me, I let him know the age difference was a little too much for me, and that while there was so much I liked about him, I didn't think we should pursue the relationship. He was shocked and angry, and his response confirmed my suspicion about the immaturity behind the emojis. That little red angry-face symbol came to life as he slammed his fist on the table. "Well, I'm sorry I wasn't good enough for you."

Lawd help me now!

He flew out of the Starbucks, and I sat at the bistro table for a moment with the entire shop looking at me. I was so glad we were in public, because it meant he had to keep himself under some modicum of control. Who knows how this would have escalated had we been at my house? I calmly got up and left, tossing my cup away. This boy then called me and accused me of breaking it off with him so I could be single for an upcoming business trip. Ladies, you'll be shocked to hear his strategy did *not* convince me to take him back. The next day, the fool tried again, bringing a dozen red roses to my office and asking me to reconsider! I gave the roses to a coworker, and he gave them to his wife. And that was the last I saw of that boy. (Until I showed him a property almost two years later. Separating business from pleasure means that, even though I may not date you, I will always sell you a house!)

It wasn't this man's age, per se, that was the problem. It was his emotional maturity. There are 20-year-old boys out there who are mature far beyond their years, and there are 60-year-olds who still manage their emotions like toddlers. Do you have time to manage a full-grown, adult toddler? I sure don't! As Power-Women, we must seek out men who are emotionally mature.

I know what you're thinking: "If that's the case, I'm never going to date again! Do emotionally mature men even exist?" Or maybe, "I'm not emotionally mature most days—how do you expect me to find a man who is?" Trust me, ladies, I've been there, and so has every single PowerWoman I know. But do not settle when it comes to this pillar.

If a man is not mature, how is he going to support you through the peaks and valleys in your life? If he hasn't reflected on his past and grown from it, how is he going to help you achieve your vision for your future? You don't need somebody who's incapable of expressing his emotions, who's going to throw fits or play games, or who is just too needy or dependent. My midsized metropolis has never been voted as the best place for singles, and the pickings aren't great. The reality is that emotionally mature men are not easy to find, but I won't budge on this pillar even a little bit.

LESSONS OF A SINGLE MOM

Many of us single moms are in the "mommy rut," and some of us are so deep in that rut that we don't have a clue when we last shaved our legs. When it comes to emotional maturity, our biggest influences these days are our children, and depending on their ages, 90% of our communication may be baby talk. So, when a real, live, adult man texts us, the sheer novelty of adult conversation makes us turn into schoolgirls, and we often put on blinders to any emotional immaturity—or other red flags—he's demonstrating. To combat this, we must look ourselves in the mirror each day and remind ourselves of the women we once were *and still are*. We are much more than PowerMoms; we are PowerWomen. When we start to view ourselves as "more than" in all areas, we will be able to discern who is a toddler and who is a man, and we will attract men with a higher level of emotional maturity. Remember, you already have children. If you marry a man who is emotionally immature, you'll have another one, and this one will never leave the nest!

Beyond being difficult to find, emotional maturity is often hard to identify, and there are a few reasons for that. If you have a history of setting the emotional maturity bar low—or if your parents or other relationship models have been emotionally immature—you may simply not know what to look for in another. If you haven't worked on your own emotional maturity, then you may not be valuing it in others. After all, we attract what we are, so when we grow ourselves, we learn what to look for in others, and people who've done their own growing start to surface in our lives.

Once you become attuned to emotional maturity in yourself and others, you'll start to recognize several characteristics that can signal maturity. For starters, emotionally mature people can have level-headed conversations about difficult topics, make decisions logically and rationally, and stick to a calendar. But most importantly, emotionally mature people can be their authentic selves with ease. Humility and vulnerability are not an issue, and they can own their shit! This seems to be difficult for the male population, so when you discover a man who discloses his flaws and failures, and who can discuss his shortcomings frankly, pay attention.

Emotionally mature men have a growth mindset and a quiet confidence about them. They are secure enough to handle intimate connection with others, and they'll demonstrate that by calling or asking you out immediately rather than hiding behind the dating app or keeping you guessing about whether they're interested. Pay attention when someone chooses to ask you questions and expresses curiosity about you rather than discussing himself. This ability to focus on others shows maturity and stability. But again, the biggest indicator of emotional maturity is when a man can admit his faults, and you can find this out on the first date with a little basic sleuthing. The question is simple: "Why are you single?" His response will tell you if he is able to own responsibility for his past and discuss his feelings without fear or if he deflects the blame onto others and sweeps his emotions under the rug.

Is there one, single standard of perfect emotional maturity? Absolutely not! Are women always emotionally mature themselves? I'm pretty sure Lorena Bobbitt answered that question a long time ago! Maturity is definitely a sliding scale, and the key is to define your own standard, hold people to that level, and spot the signs that they aren't going to make it. Take some time to reflect on your own frame of reference for emotional maturity, and then we'll take a look at some of those red flags.

*How do you search for growth in order to improve
your own emotional maturity?
What has been your frame of reference for an
emotionally mature partner?
What emotionally immature patterns have you been
shown or fallen into, yourself?*

*How can you be sure you don't settle for
those patterns again?*

INDICATOR #1:
HIDING BEHIND A SCREEN

In the last decade or so, our society seems to have replaced verbal communication with text speak and emojis, disguising emotional immaturity as cute and almost acceptable. And it's not just those "millennials" either! Every generation is guilty of this! When did it become okay to express ourselves exclusively through high-tech hieroglyphics? Ladies, this is foolproof. If a man hides behind his screen, you can bet he's not emotionally mature.

If a man wants you, and he is emotionally mature enough to express himself, he will come after you. He will quit texting and call you. He will want to hear your voice. It will drive him crazy. It is a sign of emotional maturity. When a man will only text you, it's time to question his maturity. Sure, it's scarier to pick up the phone and call someone than it is to send a quick "Hey" text message. It's harder to face potential rejection in person than on screen. But that's what separates the emotionally immature from the emotionally mature. Someone emotionally mature can be vulnerable enough to have those conversations in person. Someone emotionally mature can handle intimacy at all levels, including the art of real conversation. An emotionally mature man does not fear talking to a woman; in fact, he craves the conversation.

It is widely known that communication is key to a healthy relationship and that human beings were designed to connect with one another. But when we connect via text, we dilute that connection. We can't hear how someone's voice trembles during a difficult conversation or how a boy stumbles over his words because he's nervous about asking us out. We can't tell whether the person we're talking to is angry or sad or excited, because we can't see their facial expressions. When we communicate from behind the screen, we take the emotion out of the conversation and prevent ourselves from connecting on a deeper level.

In her book, *Conversational Intelligence*, Judith Glaser explains how our success is determined by our communication: "'To get to the next level of greatness depends on the quality of our culture, which depends on the quality of our relationships, which depends on the quality of our conversations. Everything happens through conversation." Are we relying on emojis to take us to the next level of greatness in our dating lives? In order to raise the quality of our relationships, we must raise our standards for communication.

I grew up with no call waiting, no caller ID, and no cell phones. When a boy called, chances are he spoke to one of my siblings or a parent before he spoke to me. Men in my dating demographic grew up with the same technological standards as I did, and they were trained to pick up the phone and call someone. Texting has made us much more accessible, and in many cases, that's wonderful. But it doesn't mean we can't expect old-fashioned phone calls. As you assess a man's emotional maturity, consider his generation. It stands to reason that if a man was born in 1969, he was raised with the same communication standards as I was. So if this man is only texting you—or worse, texting you with emojis instead of words—then he is not emotionally mature. A younger man may not have been raised on landlines and formal phone calls, so he may require some training in the fine art of reaching out. If he's emotionally mature, he'll embrace the opportunity. The moral of this story? Gentlemen, pick up the phone and call! We may challenge you, but we won't bite!

Just for fun, let's take this a step further. If a man wrote a letter, put it in an envelope, and mailed it to me, I might pass out due to shock. The written language in courtship is truly a lost art, and for a man to be in touch with his emotions enough to take the time and energy to write something to a woman these days is very meaningful. These are no longer the days of writing to your love while they are at war overseas, but what would it look like if we brought that type of intimacy—and that type of thoughtful effort—back to relationships?

Do not misunderstand: texting is essential in our society and in relationships. Texting is convenient, and it keeps things fun and interesting. Texting keeps a record that you can go back and read to help reignite the butterflies. And emojis can be fun too. I think they are cute, and I use them myself! But please understand that there is a difference in using emojis to be cute and fun and using them as your primary means of expressing yourself. I have known grown men to express themselves using strictly emojis. No words, just symbols. It's like looking at a poster in psychology class to pick out which face you're feeling like today! I mean, think about it: what does that eggplant emoji *really* mean?

Don't let a few texts or even emojis be the end of a budding relationship. But when a boy texts exclusively, there is an issue. If you ask him specifically to call you and he refuses, there is an issue. If he texts only in emojis, there is an issue. When my children were toddlers, I used to tell them, "Use your words!" I'd like to say the same to men today. If you think hieroglyphics are acceptable as the primary form of communication in a healthy relationship, boy, bye!

Not convinced hiding behind the screen should be a big red flag? Here's a cautionary tale from my own experience. When I got divorced there was only one dating app in our market, and it was Tinder. Yep, I joined, but don't get too excited. I was very selective, and I wouldn't go meet people without investigating them like I was the FBI. I matched with one boy who was really good looking—I mean hot!—and had a great job in medical sales. But the entire time we chatted—and even after we finally went to lunch—he never called, texted, or even sent a letter via carrier pigeon. The most advanced form of communication we had, besides Tinder, was SnapChat. I was basically a virgin to online communication, and at the time I had absolutely no clue what SnapChat was or how it operated. (In case you still haven't encountered this particular app, its party trick is that all communication disappears immediately after the other party reads it.) This man was a 37-year-old father, and he communicated exclusively via Tinder and SnapChat.

Many times, our past experiences will determine how we treat others, and he was no exception. The last time this boy had given his digits to a woman, she had decided to show up at his home unannounced in front of his child after one date. Consequently, he would no longer give any woman his phone number or address for fear of a repeat of that incident. Now, don't get me wrong: I am all for protecting our children. To call me a mama bear would be an understatement. But to never give any woman his phone number because you assume they're *all* going to show up on his doorstep? How narcissistic is that? This dude really thought he was so hot that I was going to drop whatever I was doing to drive an hour and a half to his house uninvited? Uh, that's a no, sir! But again, I understand protecting our children, so I went out with him again, thinking he needed a little more time to trust. But nothing changed, and I only Snapchatted for two weeks and two dates. If you will only communicate with me via social media, boy, bye!

As a side note, here's another reason to be cautious about SnapChat: it's popular with those of the married variety, as the disappearing conversations are far less traceable than phone records, text messages, or even emojis. But more on that later. For now, the point is, if someone will only communicate with you from behind a screen, he's probably not emotionally mature enough to rise to a PowerWoman's dating standards.

LESSONS OF A SINGLE MOM

Moms, many times the biggest excitement in our weeks is when our kids go potty! We get stuck in the "mommy minutiae," and when someone comes along to give us attention, we often take it without asking questions. But shouldn't all that toddler talk make us crave sophisticated, adult conversation even more? Especially when our kids are young, we spend our days interpreting childish drawings and partial sentences that emojis may not even register as abnormal. Remember: even if you were covered in finger-paint an hour ago, you are a hot piece of ass with an even sexier mind, and you deserve a man who can bring open, engaging, and mature conversation to the table.

When was the last time you had a really great phone call with a man?

What does healthy communication look like to you?
How can you set new communication standards
with potential partners?

INDICATOR #2:
THE D*CK PIC

The first time I received a dick pic, I was asleep early on a school night. It woke me up in more ways than one! When I told a girlfriend, of course she wanted to see the picture! But, alas, the boy had sent me his work of art via SnapChat, so it had already disappeared. It was clear, however, that he was not my match! Did this man really need his ego stroked so much that he was sending pictures of his penis all over the country via social media? Wow. Another dude, another SnapChat, another one bites the dust!

Here's the full story. I met a man on the Bumble dating app, and he was the most beautiful man I'd ever seen—in pictures or real life. This man is a professional model, and I mean that literally. He travels all over the world, and when I met him, he was in town visiting family between trips to New York and Milan. I kept singing "Jesus Loves Me" in my head the entire time I was with him. Since his time in town was limited, we went to dinner with a large group of his friends, and then we went dancing. It was a fun night of meeting and making new friends, as many of my dating app meet-ups have been, but I knew this guy and I were not a long-term match. I had no expectations of keeping in touch, but a few days later, he followed up...in a way. It was a weeknight, I had been working a lot, and I had fallen asleep early when I received a notification from Snapchat: my first dick pick! This model had decided he hadn't been photographed in the buff enough, so he'd taken a few of his own shots for me. Well, let me tell you: I know why none of the pros had been interested in photographing his dick. It was not magazine worthy.

Getting dick picks from men we hardly know has to be one of the biggest turnoffs for women of worth. Why in the world would a man think this is how to court a woman? This is no way to melt our butter, darlin'!

Timing is vital when it comes to many things in a relationship, and pictures and videos are no exception. There's no problem, inherently, with intimate photos. But the question is, when is it appropriate to share yourself with another in that way? This step requires a level of trust that usually only comes with a committed relationship. You must discern for yourself whether you desire private photos or videos to be part of your relationship and, if so, when it's the right time to introduce them. However, if a man chooses to send you pictures of himself without your consent, then sound the alarm and run!

If a man sends you pictures of himself, it's a good bet he wants you to mirror and match the behavior. If you choose to match this behavior, or if you choose to initiate this behavior, you are setting a standard for yourself and the relationship. If this is something you and your partner have discussed and are both excited about, then by all means. But if you're feeling uncertain, if you don't trust him fully, or you're considering sending intimate photos out of a sense of obligation, then girlfriend, you might want to reconsider. A man will only give you the respect you command. And besides, why undress for men when they will just undress you with their imaginations anyway? Keep in mind, a man's imagination will drive him crazy, and what he cannot see will drive his curiosity into overdrive. Yes, we should celebrate and love our bodies. But that doesn't mean we need to send intimate photos just to please a man before we're good and ready. When a boy sends me pictures of his private area or requests pictures of me, I cut him! Boy, bye!

Here's a cautionary tale: as I was writing this book, I would disclose to dates that I was writing about dating standards, and I used SnapChat as an example. One date, getting all defensive about men's proclivity to broadcast their junk all over cyberspace, chose to show me his SnapChat account in order to prove that women are equally guilty. To do this, he showed me screenshots he'd taken of a woman's explicit photos. Now, ladies, you know I have some opinions about this woman's chosen medium for her intimate pictures, but that's not the point of this particular story. The point is, I'm fairly certain that woman never intended for *me* to see her vagina. And that's what I mean when I say sharing intimate pictures requires a new level of trust. What is he going to do with them once he's got them? Will they stay private, or will he pass them around? I let this particular date know it was time for me to go home.

If you do decide to send pictures, be certain of the emotional maturity of whom you send things to. In her TED Talk, gender, sexuality, and consent researcher Amy Adele Hasinhoff points out that the concern with sexting shouldn't be around the sexts themselves but around consent.[7] We shouldn't have to receive photos we haven't consented to seeing, and all of us (and boys, I'm looking at you) need to remember that private photos do not include sharing rights unless the user gives explicit consent.

Are pictures completely off limits forever and always in a relationship? That's ultimately a decision to be made between you and your partner. If you are in a committed relationship and looking for ways to spice things up, than maybe some intimate photos are in order. But if you're concerned about the "what if's" when a relationship goes sour, then you might keep brainstorming. If you need any more advice on what *not* do when it comes to sexting, just look to Anthony Weiner.

> *Have you ever been on the receiving end of*
> *an unwanted sext?*
> *What does sexting mean to you?*
> *What are your boundaries around sexting?*
> *When is sexting appropriate for you?*

INDICATOR #3:
EXES AND UH-OHS

Another key indicator of emotional maturity (or lack thereof) is how a man handles or discusses his ex. If she seems to be hovering at the edge of every interaction you have with him, this will tip you off to his lack of emotional maturity. When a man's social media is filled with pictures of an ex, he is not ready to date. More than likely, he will also discuss her at length when you go out with him. He is still in love with her, and you are a placeholder.

The areas a man needs to work on become very clear based on how he talks about his ex. Does he become upset and angry when she comes up? Does he launch into a frustrated monologue about all the things that were wrong her? The way a man treats his former partners is a good indicator of how he'll treat you too.

So how do you know if his ex is going to be an issue? *Business Insider* suggests it is healthy to have the "ex" conversation on the first date and then consider the man's response as you decide whether to move forward.[8] (Hell yes, I take dating advice from business publications; I'm busy, and I have limited reading time.)

48

This does not have to be an in-depth conversation, but it will give you great insight as to your date's emotional status. Many break-ups are messy, but so are a lot of things in life. The key to asking a prospect about his past relationships is to discern whether or not he knows how to handle that messiness in a healthy way.

Case in point: I once went on a date with a guy who cheated on his wife and then proceeded to trash her the entire time we were at dinner. I mean, really? He should have worn a shirt that said, "Warning: Not fit for interaction with others." We had gone on approximately four dates, and the ex-wife and their marriage had been a topic of conversation every time. He told me how he'd planned the separation and arranged his finances prior to leaving in order to "win" the divorce, but he didn't divulge any responsibility he may have had for the end of the marriage. It was obvious this man had a lot of healing left to do, and he was going to use me as his therapist. And besides, if this is how he treated a woman he was committed to before his family, his child, and God, then how would he treat me? Thanks for the groceries, but I'm looking for someone who desires to cherish me, not plot against me. His emotional maturity was not in alignment with mine, so I took my leave.

If a man still has his ex at the top of his mind and the top of most of his conversations, then you need to run as fast as you can. Yes, divorce can be bitter and angry, but we must all heal and move past it before we can allow new romantic partners into our lives. Listen with intent. Are you going to be his girlfriend or his therapist? Does he blame others for the mistakes in his previous relationships, or does he also take responsibility? The reality is, no matter what the situation and no matter who is ultimately "at fault," it takes two to have a bad marriage. Make sure he can own his shit before he imposes it onto you!

How would your current (or most recent) partner's
ex describe him?
Does he ask you questions and listen, or does he
only discuss himself?
Does he admit to his faults and shortcomings?
How has he handled past relationships?
Where is his biggest area of emotional growth?

INDICATOR #4: CAN I MEET YOUR FRIENDS?

One social pattern that's very important to pay attention to when dating is your prospect's social life. How many friends does he have, and who are they? When someone can't maintain personal relationships, there is a reason. People with narcissistic tendencies do not have large groups of friends or any friends at all. Those who are not in touch with their emotions, who can't communicate well or relate with others, do not have large friend groups. Among other potential issues, if a man doesn't have many friends, you should be prepared for a clinger, as you will become the one and only person he leans on, and he will be likely to smother you early in the relationship. Close relationships with friends and family give a man stability. Without them, you may have a stage-four clinger on your hands!

You must dig deep into prospects' friend groups early to discover these issues. I recommend you start sleuthing on the first date! Asking someone to tell you about his friends and what he does for fun opens the door to loads of intel. The Singlehood can become lonely without a strong support system, so if a prospect doesn't have a friend group, it's important to find out why. It's not necessarily a red flag—maybe he's new to town—but if he refuses to answer your questions about his friends directly, dig deeper immediately.

For example, I asked a man to tell me about his friends, and he said he didn't know many people yet because he'd just moved to town. But he wouldn't say much about his circle in his old city either. Come to find out, he had moved to town two years ago. He wasn't exactly the new kid on the block. So, on the next date, I dug deeper: "Who do you spend time with?" He told me about his meetings with his pastors, his therapist, and his life group at church. There was clarity. There was more to this than being new in town; there was some kind of instability there, and there were patterns of trauma in his world. I knew then that it was time for me to walk away.

Sometimes it can be difficult to self-protect by walking away when you have a heart to help others, but you must remember to protect yourself and your children as well. The lack of friendships in a prospect's world can reflect deeper issues, and while those issues may not be deal breakers, you must ask fierce questions in order to both help the person across from you and protect yourself. Remember: if someone isn't your fit, that only means they are someone else's fit; by walking away, you're providing that opportunity.

It's easy to learn about someone's capacity to build relationships in the very beginning by asking about his habits and his schedule. How does he fill his time, and whom does he spend it with? EHarmony breaks down the need for friendships before romantic relationships in order to prevent codependency as well as other possible relationship issues.[9] The main question is, if someone is not able to make and maintain long-term relationships in other areas of his life, how will he be able to have a healthy long-term relationship with you? If he texts you constantly and he's available to be with you every waking hour of every day, then you may want to look for somebody with more relationships in his life, who won't rely solely on you. Likewise, what do the relationships in *your* life look like, and are you ready for a long-term romantic relationship?

I thought I had found Mr. Right. He owned his own business, he held doors open for me, and his values aligned with mine, but he seemed to want to spend every waking hour with me after our first date. I had just entered the Singlehood, so it took me a minute to figure out his patterns—because when we are new to the Singlehood, we are just happy to have the attention. At first, I couldn't see past the instability. If he didn't have his children, he wanted to be at my side every night of the week. He didn't seem to have any hobbies, friends, or clubs, and he didn't even seem to enjoy alone time. When we weren't together, this dude would text me all day, every day. Once I recognized the pattern, I knew to dig deeper. When I asked him about who his friends were, I'll never forget his response: "My ex-wife got all the friends in the divorce." Yes, it was wonderful to feel wanted again, but it was a little too telling that his ex-wife had been the one holding all the relationships together. This man's statement told me everything, and I ended things immediately. Now, don't get me wrong, I'm flattered when someone wants to spend all their time with me! As PowerWomen, we're obviously worth that kind of attention. But, ladies, we've got things to do and places to be! We don't have time to dedicate all day to these men, and we should look for men whose lives are equally full and fulfilling.

Likewise, the kind of people a man surrounds himself with

will tell you a lot about his character. Who we surround ourselves with says something about who we are, and we should pay very close attention to this in dating. Does he choose to associate with people who have strong values, or does he post pictures of his friends' mug shots on social media? I went out with a very kind man for a few weeks before we started talking about his friends. Being born and raised in the area, I knew the guys he hung around with, and I knew their reputations and their pasts did not align with my own values. This man didn't seem to be like those guys on the surface, but I knew he must align with him if they were his best buddies, and they weren't people I wanted to surround myself with. It is difficult to fully understand a person's character early on in a relationship, but looking at whom he surrounds himself with can be very telling.

What does a healthy social life look like to you?
What does your current (or most recent) partner's social life look like?
Has he been able to maintain close relationships for a long period of time?
Do you want to spend time with his friends?

LESSONS OF A SINGLE MOM

As parents, we often want to choose whom our children are friends with because we know how much those friends will influence them. As dating parents, we can model this by actually choosing whom we surround our children with. Remember, your partner will eventually want you and your children around his friends, his kids, his parents, etc. Do his friends support a lifestyle you want for your children? As parents, we are always the models for our children, and the people we embrace as "friends" set a standard for the type of company they should keep and the behavior they should find acceptable. How do you want your partners and their friends to influence your children?

How do we find people who are emotionally mature? What is the secret sauce? The key is knowing what this standard looks like for you and building up your own emotional maturity. We have to meet our own standards before we will find partners who do. The more we heal and grow within ourselves, and the more comfortable we become being single, the more emotionally mature men will show up in our world.

Regardless of when or whether a man comes along, what is most important is that you are becoming an amazing, self-confident, and self-reliant woman who can feel sexy dancing in your underwear in your bedroom! When we choose to speak love into ourselves and build our inner strength, then we're inviting emotionally mature men to join us.

What were the emotional standards in your
previous relationships?
How are you becoming emotionally mature
in order to attract another?
How are you maintaining emotional standards
in your dating life?

THREE

Never "Just a _____"

After my divorce, I lacked direction in every part of my life. But when I discovered business coaching a month after the divorce, I found structure, discipline, guidance, mentorship, innovation, bold thinking, and encouragement that I had never experienced before. My first business coach was a man who was not a fit for me, but the next five coaches I had were women who completely changed my life. Having a business coach was better than having a spouse in many ways, as I was learning to lean on myself for the first time.

The coaching structure that best fit me and my vision included regular one-on-one coaching with group coaching sessions once a year. During a group course, the coach requested I share my journey with the class. I stood up and opened with "I'm just a single mom." Right then, only a few seconds into my introduction, the coach interrupted me with the words that would change my life: "*No!* You are not *just* a single mom, you are a PowerMom!"

Why should anything—motherhood, our marital or dating status, or anything else—define our lives? I am so much more than a mom. I am so much more than a single mom. I'm more than a realtor, I'm more than a daughter, and I'm more than a woman! When we define ourselves by just one of our titles, we limit our views of ourselves and stifle our growth. There's precedent for that, of course: historically, single women were defined by their eligibility, and married women were defined by their husbands. Back then, we didn't even get to identify with our own names! And today, we still allow ourselves to be defined by our motherhood, our careers, or our relationship status too often. Until we choose to view ourselves more holistically, why should we expect anyone else to view us as more than "just" any one title?

Since the divorce, I had limited myself by focusing my worth on single motherhood, so I had never opened my mind to think of other opportunities. My limited mindset had limited my potential, and I had been using the term "single mom" as a crutch to stay comfortable with my limitations. I had been avoiding the expectation to rise up and fulfill my potential. I was living in the land of excuses. But the moment my coach said those words, I started to define my purpose. I no longer defined myself as "just" anything. I was much more, as all of us are. We are PowerWomen! When we shift our mindsets and eliminate "just" from our vocabularies, opportunities start to show up.

What is your value proposition? As women, we throw the word "worth" around with each other quite a bit, yet we rarely focus on what it really means for us. What if we looked at our worth through the lens of what makes us unique? Our drive to conform develops early, but we should be celebrating our individuality and uniqueness, because that is where our true value and power lie. We are worth what we offer to the world, so we should define our worth based on our uniqueness. No one wrote articles on Joan Rivers's perspective of global climate change, because her unique value is in other spaces, and she embraced that value.

Likewise, Hillary Clinton isn't hosting a television show about sex, fashion, and celebrities, because her unique value lies elsewhere. (And I'd be willing to bet neither woman ever used the word "just" to describe her own expertise or talents.) If we all offered the same gifts, we wouldn't have any value. Our power is in our uniqueness, and the sooner we celebrate that, the more joy we will find and the more we will be able to create change for others. Consequently, when we make the choice to raise our standards and our opinions of our own value, men have no option than to treat us differently.

If you don't know where to start identifying your unique value, think about your "why" in life. What makes your feet hit the floor in the morning and gets you excited about the day? What drives you? What is your passion? These are key aspects of your unique value. To be a woman in a male-dominated world is a challenge. Our feet have to hit the floor with a little more than passion and a stronger sense of "why" some days; that "why" shows us our value and gives us the grit and strength to persevere.

A woman will struggle to be in a healthy relationship until she knows her true value, and that means knowing how to love her whole self, see her full potential, and demand that others recognize her worth too. From an amazingly young age, women are taught that we are to be a certain size, act a certain way, get married, have children, and die without ever stepping out of line, challenging the status quo, or showing any sort of pride in our accomplishments. I don't know about you, but I've got more on my agenda than that! But when a woman fully loves all of who she has become, she becomes labeled a dangerous woman! (Cue Ariana Grande!)

I had the privilege to attend the 2019 World Women's Summit

and learn about PowerWoman Pat Mitchell, who went from broke single mother to media mogul. She is the former President of CNN, current editorial director of TEDWomen, and author of *Becoming a Dangerous Woman*. In a commencement speech she gave at the University of Miami in 2019, she encouraged the women in the audience to become dangerous, and by that she meant fearless: "using and sharing your power to empower others … becoming an active, engaged, and informed participant in the shaping of a better world than the one you are entering today."[10] A woman like Mitchell describes doesn't sound dangerous to me. She sounds like a PowerWoman who has discovered her own unique value!

How does knowing our value affect our choices in dating? Once we discover what we're worth, then we can invite someone else to sit across the table from us because we see equal or more value in them. And more importantly, we can demand that whoever's sitting at our table see and respect the value we have to offer. On the other hand, when we don't see our own value, or when we let society define our value for us, it can be easy to settle. As little girls, we are told we can go anywhere, do anything, and be anyone we choose to become (never mind the constant barrage of fairytales training us to become little more than damsels in distress). Then that childhood dream disappears, and many of us find ourselves in careers we hate or relationships that don't work, wearing the same haircut for twenty years. I mean, how are women to view our value in a society where, despite the 1963 Equal Pay Act, we still make $0.79 for every $1.00 a man earns? What if we saw the potential we were told about when we were younger? What if we never stopped dreaming? What if we didn't allow anything to limit us? What if we made our own fairytales?

What if we started out as dangerous girls instead of waiting until we'd hit bottom to become dangerous women? What change would that elicit?

You are strongest when you love yourself and know you are worthy to receive the love others offer and the opportunities life presents. And once you find your inner strength and worth, use it to find a man who's ready to celebrate and match it.

What is unique to your journey, and how are you
sharing that to empower others?
How are you showing yourself love?
How do you define yourself?
What would you accomplish if you didn't fear anything?

KNOW YOUR WORTH

So many women do not realize the power they hold, and that prohibits them from attracting the right kind of man (not to mention countless other amazing opportunities). But when you align yourself with your purpose and know your priorities, men will see your confidence, and they will show up on your doorstep like pretty little packages from Amazon! And you'll get to choose which ones to unwrap and which ones to return.

Do you know your value proposition? Do you know what you bring to the table? To a man, your value proposition is what you see in yourself. Do you view yourself as priceless, or do you minimize your value? Forbes suggests that because women do not know our valuation, we are consequently being undervalued and underpaid in the workplace.[11] In other words, we aren't commanding equal pay because we don't realize what we bring to the table. Are we doing this in the dating space too? Are we lowering our standards because we don't recognize our true value? When you see and know your own value, you'll finally get the return on investment you have been waiting for: self-happiness. If you thought I was gonna say a man, that's a no, ma'am! The right men will see it too, but they're just a bonus.

"Morning Joe" cohost Mika Brzezinski's book, *Know Your Value: Women, Money and Getting What You're Worth*, is a brilliant guide to figuring out what we're worth! Brzezinski explains how women are excellent at knowing when their stock is low but not recognizing when their stock is high, and she gives examples of how she settled when she should have been demanding more, because she didn't recognize her valuation. To recognize her own value, the question Brzezinski had to ask herself was, "What would 'Morning Joe' look like without me on it?" Her absence showed her valuation, and she realized her stock was high. Once we have clarity on who we are, our valuation, what makes us tick, and our worth as women, we will no longer fear having fierce conversations. Learning to recognize that our stock is high allows us to step into the conversations authentically and ask for a raise, lay out our dating standards, or anything else. Because let's be honest: when we know what we're worth, we're empowered to ask for whatever we want!

Unfortunately, most men are not prepared for the conversations, nor are they prepared for women to be fierce. Often men's negative reactions to our confidence lead us to shove that value way back down inside us. But really, what they're showing us is that they're afraid of our strength, so we should use their discomfort as an invitation to keep on climbing. So, stand firm in who you are. If he's worth your time, he'll respect and admire that.

Our power as women is equal to the power any man has, and we should use it to build the professional, personal, and dating lives we want. So many men are afraid of a strong woman. Well, darlin', if he's afraid of your strength, you haven't met the right man.

Women are willing to stand up for our friends, our families, and those in need. Why are we not willing to stand up for ourselves? It may be because our society doesn't stand up for us when we need it the most. Others show how much they value us during our times of greatest need, and, for women, that external value has never been high. For example, we have been disregarded when we have spoken out about sexual assault. Just look at the backlog of rape kits across the country: the number of untested kits in the United States is reported to be in the hundreds of thousands.[12] How are women to feel valued when we muster the courage to speak up during our most vulnerable times, only for society and the government to dismiss us and our trauma?

Even when we think we know our value, it can be all too easy to let someone else's value blind us to what we're worth. There are times when we see a man's worth so clearly it scares us. We know how much he brings to the table, and we fear he will get away and we won't find someone like him again. Panic sets in, and we start pandering to his value instead of upholding ours. We do things like text desperately and cling for our lives, and then we wonder what scared him off. We don't demand that he value or respect us as much as we value him, and it backfires. I've fallen into this trap, and so have many PowerWomen I know. That's why my girl-friends and I have an agreement: when we feel the urge to reach out to a boy, we must text or call each other instead. Whatever you do, *do not* chase a man! When a man truly desires you, he will take action. My papa taught me this, remember? He'll even travel states away and get you out of prison to be with you!

It's so tempting, when we're feeling insecure about our value, to continually text and call men for any reason we can think of. Resist! Don't be like the clingers we talked about in the last chapter. Remember that your life is complete and fulfilling whether that man is in it or not, so there's no need to chase him down. Know that the man you are supposed to be with has perfect timing. When he sees you, he will come after you with everything he has. Keep the faith. You are worthy of a man who sees all of your valuation! In other words, remember that you are a hot piece of ass and a rare commodity in the dating space! *He* is the one who has reason to be intimidated by *your* value—not the other way around. If not, well, he is only one Amazon package; rest assured another one will come along. Let go of the fear, embrace your value, and have faith that the right man will see and appreciate all that you are!

When I entered the Singlehood, I had failed at so many things. But mostly, I had never taken the time to learn who I *was* as opposed to who I was *expected to be*. I had to go through a major life change and some incredibly difficult times to gain a new perspective. Now, I have allowed myself time to discover who I am, what I have to offer, and what makes me tick. By loving myself enough to learn what makes me smile in life, I discovered just how valuable I am to others too.

What do you love most about yourself?
How would your best friends describe you?
What are you doing to love yourself?

WHAT IS YOUR HOURLY RATE?

I had agreed to meet a guy for coffee, and the first thing I noticed when he walked in was that he looked older than his pictures. He wasn't catfishing exactly, but he wasn't being fully honest online either. I knew immediately that this wasn't going anywhere. I had no plans to sit there long enough to enjoy a coffee, so I grabbed a free water. He talked the entire time—nervous dude chatter all about his retirement—and he made sure to point out his convertible. He was a definite no, ma'am! Just as I was strategizing a graceful way out, I got a call from another dude, thank goodness. I made my excuses, thanked him for his time, and left. The date didn't last more than fifteen minutes, but that was fine with me. I have too much going on to waste more than fifteen minutes, and sometimes even that can be too much.

Listen, I'm busy, and I know my hourly rate. It's not easy to build time into the day for a date when you run a business, are a committed and involved mother, provide the only stream of income for the family, and enjoy time with friends and family. Hell, you're lucky if you can hold my attention long enough for a text message, much less a date! If I allow time for you, you must be special. (Ladies, any man you want to attract will have this same mindset. He is busy and focused. If he wants you, then he makes time for you. If he makes time for you, then he wants you!)

Time is our most valuable commodity. We cannot replace time. We cannot go backward in time. We cannot go forward in time. Once we've given our time, then it's gone. So, truly ask yourself, "What is your time worth?" If you make a product, it takes time to produce it. If you are salaried, you are paid for your time based on your expertise in a given field. If you are an independent contractor, you are paid for the hours you work. If you value volunteering, your friends, family, hobbies, or travel, how do you prioritize these things in your limited time? Every time we say yes to something, we say no to something else. It costs us. How do we ensure the things we say yes to are worth the cost?

What is your hourly rate? How much is your time worth? Is he really worth the time it takes to go out to dinner? When you start looking at dating this way, you realize who gets your attention and who doesn't! When the date goes badly and you realize you could have been paid a lot more for that hour than the cost of the dinner, that perspective is so powerful! Why go to dinner with somebody you aren't that interested in or who doesn't meet your standards if it will probably be a waste of precious time? I will gladly pay for dinner and leave rather than endure any time with a man who isn't worth my time.

Sometimes there's validation in conversation. I was in a group text with several realtors in my market, one of who was a hot, single guy. Suddenly the conversation took an interesting turn:

Me: Hey, y'all need a rental? I just listed a fine piece of ass in SWLR for $75k that is in perfect shape to rent for at least $800/month!

Hot Dude: Your body or your rent house?!?

Me: Darlin', I'm a lot more than $800/month

Hot Dude: I was gonna say…

So, I picked up the phone and called the hot dude.

Me: What the hell are you doing commenting on my hourly rate?

Dude: (laughing) I was just clarifying.

Me: Since you brought it up, what would you estimate

my hourly rate to be?

Dude: Are you kidding me? You're more like $2,500 for a moment!

Me: No, no. We should all view ourselves like we view our children, and I view my children as priceless.

When enough men treat you like a hooker, you'll quickly gain clarity on your hourly rate and learn how to command the treatment you want and deserve. I was shocked to learn that the current going rate for a hooker is $260 per hour.[13] So a woman who is paid this same rate and works a forty-hour week would gross $41,600 per month and $500,000 a year. (To add some perspective, in my state, we just increased the minimum wage to $12 per hour.) This quick math truly places a value on the pussy! I got really clear on this concept when I matched with a man on the Bumble dating app. I had been single a few years, and he was a Fortune 500 executive with many accolades he enjoyed bragging about. He was visiting town and asked me to dinner. We met, and the conversation was forced, but the groceries were good. The server came by, and he requested two checks. This didn't surprise me too much, because we were not a fit. I was happy to pay for my dinner. But then he had the gall to ask me to come back to his hotel room. If the going rate for a hooker is $260 an hour, I must have seemed like a bargain! Much to his disappointment, I declined and went home immediately, because my hourly rate is beyond his imagination—especially with behavior like that. Darlin', if you are going to treat me like a hooker, you'd better be prepared to pay me like one! Since I'm a realtor and an entrepreneur, let's put this in business terms. What does the dating market look like? Is it a buyer's or seller's market? What does the competition look like? Is inventory scarce or overstocked? If you know your hourly rate and you know how much time you're spending on someone, then you can calculate your ROI, or your return on investment. Is he worth the investment? There is such power in knowing this! When you know your hourly rate, it becomes so much easier to say yes or no to whatever possibilities come along. You work hard for the money, honey! Own it, know it, and place an extreme value on it! Ask yourself, "Is he $500 hot or $100 hot?" "Is he $100 aligned with my values or $1,000?" When you gain clarity in this area, you will be able to cut through the pickup lines and respond with a confident "yes" or "no, thank you."

When we change our mindsets about how we spend our time, whom we give it to, and how we manage it, that's when we realize our total freedom of choice in the dating world. Get a clear vision of where your time is most valuable, and focus on those areas. Do we have to reach wage equality in order to command higher standards in the dating space? No. Despite the wage gap, I'm clear that the value of a woman is equal to or higher than that of a man in any position. So don't wait on our male-driven society to determine your value. Set your own standards and stay focused, and you will start to attract right-minded people. When they start to flock, you'll get to choose!

Knowing your hourly rate enables you to enjoy life on your own and empowers you to make fulfilling decisions for yourself. When I started going to nice dinners with girlfriends, it made it easier to say no to dinners with dudes I didn't care to spend time with. When I started traveling on my own, with my children, and with girlfriends, it became easier to pass up trips with men because I didn't need them to provide those opportunities. I empowered myself by learning my hourly rate.

The most important thing any of us has to give is our time, and we should all know the value of our time before we allow anyone to freely take it.

Who do you value the most in your world?
Are you valuing yourself the same way?
What is your hourly rate?

DEMAND RESPECT

I was going to have surgery, and when I met my doctor for the initial consultation, he asked what I do for a living, and before you knew it, I had an appointment to list his house after my surgery. The sale was forced due to his recent divorce, and he was dating a woman who was almost twenty years younger than he was, so I can't tell you how surprised I was when he said, "So you're going to sell my house, but after surgery I'll have one up on you: I will have already been inside you." I was shocked, but I shut him down fast and hard: "That's a good try, but unfortunately for you it's not going to work. See you for surgery." Ladies, it's these kinds of encounters that give single men a bad reputation! Luckily for him, he was an excellent doctor—otherwise he might've lost my business as well as my respect. After my surgery, I sold his house in less than a week and sold him a new house shortly thereafter. I might not date you, but I'm happy to take your money.

There is a breed of men for whom being sleazy feels successful. With this breed, the term "sexual harassment" is an understatement. The slimy approach has worked in the past, so they feel as if they can say anything and get away with it. At least, until they meet a woman who won't stand for it! I have had men tell me

"I want to eat you" and "get in your cunt" in the workplace. Yes, they've had success with these disgusting pick-up lines, so they keep using them. Please, ladies, don't encourage this behavior! Boys, I will not waste my time suffering from the manners your mama didn't teach you! Remember, the way he treats you when he's first trying to get your attention says a lot about how he'll treat you once you're dating him. If he shows this utter lack of respect right off the bat, it's never going to get better. Ladies, raise your standards, and mothers, teach your sons manners so we can break the chain of misogyny!

Too often, we are only seen for our exterior, whatever that may look like. When that happens, we get to choose how we respond and how we carry ourselves in order to be heard. That is where our power lies! God put both beauty and brains in our toolboxes, and we are to use them to our full advantage. If a man chooses to see you as an object, then outsmart him! After all, your IQ will always be higher than your cup size!

Women are rising throughout the country, and one of the biggest manifestations of that is the #MeToo movement. This is also, unfortunately, one of the most disturbing illustrations of just how often men objectify women rather than seeing the full picture. Actress Alyssa Milano brought Tarana Burke's #MeToo movement to the forefront of global awareness in 2017 with a single tweet: "If all the women who have ever been sexually harassed or assaulted wrote 'Me too' as a status, we might give people a sense of the magnitude of the problem." The domino effect on social media and in all other areas of our culture was astounding as women came together in support of other women after the Harvey Weinstein sexual abuse allegations. Unfortunately, out of the five million Americans who experience sexual harassment each year, only 9,200 file charges with the EOCC. That means 99.8% of cases go unreported.[14, 15]

Men have a lot of work to do on themselves to fix their mindsets and change their behavior. There's no doubting that. But, ladies, we don't have time to sit around and wait for them to figure their shit out—we have to take action! When we understand our worth as full, complex human beings—and we bring that full value to every interaction—*then* we can teach men to respect us for all that we bring to the table. The law of attraction states that you attract what you put out into the universe. If you want a person of worth, put yourself out there as someone of worth. If you post selfie after selfie in not much more than a bathing suit and a duck face, you'll attract men who aren't looking for much more than that. The duck-face selfie may represent one facet of your amazing personality, but that's the thing: it's *just one facet*. Show it off, sure, but remember to show the world all the other incredible things you're made of! For an example of what I'm talking about, consider Cady Heron in the masterpiece, *Mean Girls*. What is she bringing into her life when her sole focus is on fitting in with the popular crowd? What about when she rocks her intelligence as well as her looks? (Hello, great grades, good friends, and Aaron Samuels.) You have to align how you behave with what you know you're worth, the kind of respect you're looking for in a man, and the kind of relationship you want. When we are disappointed with what we attract, it makes looking in the mirror that much more difficult. But we must continue to hold ourselves and our sisters accountable for raising the standards for how we will let others treat us.

The misogyny of the older male population is slowly dissolving as younger generations move up in the world, but that doesn't mean we no longer face the same challenges. When you know your hourly rate and what you bring to the table, there is no longer a question of whether you will tolerate sexual harassment—or any kind of belittling behavior from men—in the workplace, the dating space, or anywhere else in your life.

What level of respect are you demanding?

MAKE YOURSELF A PRIORITY

I've chosen to leave my ex-husband out of this book because we are raising children together. This one involves him, that's true, but it is much more about me than about him. A couple of years after my second child was born, I still had a lot of leftover "baby weight." It didn't help that I had been choosing to eat and drink whatever I wanted and neglecting to exercise. But I finally grew tired of my muffin top and my control top, and I started losing the baby weight. It was clear that I had been prioritizing everyone in my life except me, and my then-husband's comment solidified that pattern: "Thank you for losing the weight for me." Well, ladies, that opened my eyes in a big way! I was teaching my entire family how to treat me based on the way I treated myself, and I had not been treating myself with respect or commanding it from anyone else. If I didn't show myself respect and love through self-care, then why should anyone else?

In order to make it in the Singlehood (or any phase in life, really), we must prioritize our own self-care. As women, we tend to be terrible about taking care of ourselves. Self-care is not an innate behavior, though caring for everyone around us sure seems to be. We must condition ourselves to care for ourselves, recognizing our needs and fulfilling them for ourselves. After all, why would someone make you a priority in their life if you don't make yourself a priority in your own life?

It took my girlfriends dressing me to go to the club for me to realize I was still wearing maternity underwear even though I hadn't been pregnant in four years. Motherhood is delicious, there's no doubt, but I had lost myself in it, and it had overshadowed everything else about me. Before I knew it, almost everything I wore and did identified me as "just" a mother. Now, I take time to develop other aspects of my life, and I find myself going to buy lingerie even when I'm not in a relationship, just because it makes me feel good. And guess what? Taking better care of myself like this means I have the energy and the mindset to take even better care of my children.

It is vital to care for yourself in order to care for others and to show others how to care for you. What causes you to laugh the most, relax the most, and reflect the most? What brings you the most joy? How are you purposeful in finding your joy? What are you feeding yourself? Who are you surrounding yourself with? What are you listening to? How are you caring for your body? When is the last time you had a massage, hot bath, or time alone? Are you meditating or having quiet time? When is the last time you bought a nice dress that made you feel good walking into a room? When was the last time you did something you rarely do for yourself? Evaluate these questions on a weekly basis to hold yourself accountable for your self-care. You may need to check several times a week, or even daily, to maintain motivation, clarity, and sanity.

Remember that hourly rate we talked about? How we need to be choosy about who we give our time to? Well, sister, you deserve your own time more than anyone else, so learn to share your most precious commodity freely with the woman looking back at you in the mirror. It takes work to retrain your brain to care for yourself first, but when we start to give ourselves the same love and respect we show others, we'll be ready to receive it in return.

What aspects of your life are not reflecting who you are?
How is that showing up in the rest of your world?
How are you showing yourself respect? If you aren't, how
could you be?

LESSONS OF A SINGLE MOM

A recent Huffington Post article says it best: "If I'm going to lose my self [sic] for a decade, motherhood sure is a delicious thing to lose it to."[16] When our children are infants, toddlers, and sometimes even adolescents, we can completely lose ourselves as we pour everything we have into them. As single PowerMoms, our resources are limited, and we often choose to give everything to our children instead of caring for ourselves. If there is a choice between shopping for school supplies or getting a pedicure, we will always choose the school supplies. But modeling self-care by displaying healthy eating habits, journaling, nurturing positive friendships, exercising, and bringing laughter into your home will be more impactful for your children than any one outfit you may buy them.

Do you treat yourself the way you want your daughter to treat herself as an adult? Show your children you are worthy of self-care, so they will develop the same confidence in themselves.

So many times we are distracted by what we have to say no to instead of focusing on what we are saying yes to in our lives. What if every breakup or tough moment was viewed as a yes? "Yes, I'm better than this," "Yes, I refuse to settle," "Yes, I know my value proposition," "Yes, I am perfectly capable of surviving—and thriving—alone," and "Yes, I am worthy of a love far beyond my imagination!" Start saying yes to the good in life! Yes to loving yourself, yes to being treated how you deserve to be treated, yes to what is important in your world, yes to your values, yes to surrounding yourself with people who lift you up, yes to pouring into others, yes to your children, and, most importantly, yes to you!

Finding Your North Star

A couple of years ago, I had traveled to a coaching training four hours away, and I was at dinner with a man who was much older than me and in a corporate leadership position within my company. He was divorced, had adult children, and had been in the Singlehood going on ten years. We discussed our company, our faith, and our values, and then dating came up. Listening to him describe how he wanted to court a woman was fascinating to me. It was my first time hearing a man of character talk about seeking a mate with intention. He told me about what he looked for in a partner and how, when he found her, he wanted to pursue her completely, with no desire to seek others. Why did he have to be my parents' age? As most single girls will tell you, the good ones are off-limits! In this case, he was too old based on the parameters I'd set for myself. Instead of compromising my own standards, I sat in awe of the example this man was setting for me.

I was frustrated then, and continued to be disappointed for a while, that I wasn't attracting men of character who were appropriate for me in age, marital status, or sexual orientation. But eventually I learned that I wasn't attracting these men because I wasn't allowing "strong character" into my world. I didn't know what I valued in relationships, nor did I have a firm handle on what I valued for myself. But through more breakdowns came more breakthroughs, and I was able to grow. I took time for myself, away from dating, and I identified my top ten values. I focused on them and journaled around them, and when I was ready to date again, men who reflected my values started to show up in my world. Once again, I had choices.

Ladies, look for a man who knows what he stands for, what he values, and what he believes. But more importantly, know what *you* stand for, what *you* value, and what *you* believe. Your values are your North Star and your guiding light that inform every decision you make. When a man's values and principles align with yours, it creates a magic that sustains the relationship. Your top ten values may be different from mine, and that's okay. But there are three that I think every woman should consider carefully: respect, integrity, and faith. When you can build a relationship on respect, integrity, and similar faith journeys (whatever those may be), your energy together will be amazing, and you'll find you have a stronger shared focus and drive than when your values are out of alignment. When you know what you're looking for in terms of values like respect, integrity, and faith, and when you know what is most important to you, then you'll be able to recognize whether he is prepared to support your mission and vision—and whether you want to support his.

LESSONS OF A SINGLE MOM

Dating around a work schedule, a social calendar, *and* your children's needs can be difficult. Every single parental situation is different, but the question I always ask myself when considering someone as a long-term partner is, "Does this man set the example I want for my children?" If the answer is yes, then continue with curiosity. The minute you answer no, cut him. If he is not good enough for your children, then he is not worth your time. To be real clear: if at any time you don't see yourself ever being comfortable introducing him to your children, then cut him. When we introduce someone to our children, we are showing our sons how they should treat women and our daughters how they should behave and expect to be treated. I've been in the Singlehood since 2015, and I've yet to introduce anyone to my children. The rules around this look different for each of us, but I've decided that I need a committed future with a partner before I allow my children to enter the courtship. What dating experience do you want to model for your children? What dating expectations do you have for your children? Do you want another's values to influence your children?

R.E.S.P.E.C.T:
FIND OUT WHAT IT MEANS TO YOU!

The phrase should be, "*Beside* every PowerMan is a PowerWoman, and *beside* every PowerWoman is a PowerMan." In a healthy relationship, no woman is ever *behind* a man, and no man is ever *behind* a woman. Relationships are partnerships, and a man and a woman should walk side-by-side in their greatness. As a PowerWoman, you must commit to a true partnership, complete with peaks and valleys in which you take turns celebrating, encouraging, and supporting one another. This type of partnership is not for the weak. You have to consistently recommit to each other, just as athletes do on the field. And the way I see it, the foundation of this kind of side-by-side partnership is deep, unshakeable mutual respect.

Once you've established that mutual respect, each of you will have pride for the other and support one another in all endeavors, because you'll both support the same mission and vision for your family. It will be easy to allow your partner to lead when needed, and it will be easy for him to hand over the reins to you when he needs guidance. You will encourage and support one another in every area of your lives. It sounds ideal, doesn't it? Of course, these days, what is most difficult is finding a man who is both single *and* worthy of our respect.

After a year-long hiatus from online dating, I decided to give it another shot. I matched with a man who was decent looking, and we had fantastic conversation. He asked me to dinner, but I wasn't very optimistic. He lived on a farm thirty minutes away from me, and he had moved his parents next door. He had amazing family values, and I respected him a great deal, but I knew we were not a fit. He talked me into dinner anyway, and my suspicions were correct. When I asked him what his ideal married life looked like, he described life on the farm. He expected a life with fairly traditional gender roles, and he couldn't understand my passion for women's empowerment. He didn't respect my values, I didn't agree with his, and I was not going to be the little woman on the farm. We hugged it out after dinner, and we both moved on.

As women, we always need to ask high-level, value-oriented questions as we seek out our partners. This particular clash of values—over "traditional" versus "progressive" gender roles—is one I've seen over and over again. It seems as though we continue the conversation about equality in the workplace and society in general, but we don't talk much about equality at home. Traditionally, women are in charge of the housework, and this has persisted even as women have taken the workforce by storm. But there's more: Eve Rodsky's book, *Fair Play*, discusses gender roles at home and cites study after study that find men do *even less work* at home after children arrive. Women's roles continue to expand, while men's shrink. Is that what you expect in your home? How are you laying out the expectations with your conversations?

What I have found in the Singlehood is that many of the men who have been on their own—breadwinners, PowerParents, men of quality—also have a grasp of what it takes to "do it all," and they have an extreme appreciation for a woman's ability to juggle. With these men, laundry and dishes are small things, and no one cares to argue over who is assigned these tasks. He'll wash the dishes without a word, and so will we. The focus, once we're in relationships with PowerMen, is on the big picture, on the joy of life, on each other, on how we want the children to grow, how we want to give back to others, and how we want to enjoy one another. The PowerMan knows and understands the struggle, and it's easy to form immediate and deep respect with this breed.

Whether your respect gap is in gender roles or anything else, it can be disheartening to see the same missed connection over and over. How do you find someone who will be fully committed to your vision?

When you talk to men, one of the things they'll tell you they crave the most from failed relationships is respect from a partner. But it's not only men who crave respect—PowerWomen crave it, too, and we view demonstrations of respect as acts of love. We all choose to respect others in different ways and for different reasons, but one key sign of respect in a relationship is each partner's willingness and eagerness to celebrate one another. Ladies, applauding a man in front of others because you truly admire him is not a sign of weakness or pandering but a reflection of the respect you, as a PowerWoman, desire and deserve as well. PowerMen will do the same for the women they respect. We should all seek ways—within our pillars and values—to earn the continuous respect of our partners in our relationships, and we should also continuously seek to applaud our partners as demonstrations of our love. Let others hear us praise our partners and think, "Wow, what a happy relationship!" We know it is much more than a happy relationship—it's one built on love and respect.

What causes you to respect a man?
How do you show respect in your relationships?
How do you want a partner to show his respect for you?

There is a confirmed bachelor in my town who has texted me a few times over the years. Keep in mind, these texts have only come after ten p.m., and we are not close friends. Based on their timing, these texts can only imply one thing. And to corroborate that theory, I've heard reports from a few of his neighbors about how many different women leave his house in the early morning hours as they recount the walk of shame. But I won't play his game. I'm not a girl of the night—I'm the girl at the top of a man's mind first thing in the morning. I have made it a habit to humble this boy by responding to him when I wake up at 5:30 a.m.

instead of when he reaches out at night. You teach people how to treat you with respect, and they grow into your expectations.

And speaking of humbling boys, a man's humility is a powerful indicator of his capacity to respect a partner. I have discovered that many of the fish in this sea are pretty—real pretty—but they've never developed a set of values or a belief system that keeps them humble. Can you please get past your pretty?! Maybe it's your face, or maybe it's your bank account, but darlin', that pretty does not impress me by itself, and it's not unique, either. Give me five minutes, and I'll show you another man who's just as pretty or just as wealthy as you, if not more so. John Mayer said it best in a 2017 tweet: "If you're pretty, you're pretty; but the only way to be beautiful is to be loving. Otherwise, it's just 'congratulations about your face.'"[17]

It is so important to see how a man maintains his humility, because it's only when we are humble that we have the capacity to truly respect somebody else. We can be confident, of course, and we should seek confident men. But when confidence gives way to self-obsession, that's a red flag. If Mr. Gorgeous's profile is full of shirtless pictures, that should give you pause. If Mr. Banks feels the need to discuss his private jet during your first conversation, that should give you pause too. When he is humble, he will be able to think of himself less often and prioritize you. When he is humble, he will be curious about you, what interests you, and all things that make you tick. Martin Luther says it beautifully: "Whatever your heart clings to and confides in, that is really your God." Does he cling to the gym, work, himself, family, faith, a belief system? What keeps him humble? How does he make room for someone else in his worldview?

FIRST IMPRESSIONS AREN'T ALWAYS ACCURATE

My first impression of the late-night-texter was right, but there've been plenty of times when my first impressions have been wrong. When we meet someone online or learn about someone from friends, we don't often get the whole picture. And in-person meetings can lead to surprises of both the positive and negative variety. I matched with a man on a dating app and, after three weeks of phone conversations and laughter, he drove three hours to take me to dinner. Interestingly enough, his phone personality was much better than his in-person personality. He arrived in town the morning of the date, rather than in the evening as we'd planned, but since he'd seemed promising, I rearranged my schedule and made time. Immediately, I learned his friends had nicknamed me a "man-eater" solely based on my pictures. I offered suggestions as to what we could do that day, but he disregarded every one of them and chose his own activities. He complained about my city, made racial remarks, and discussed how he wanted to remarry and bring someone back home to live with him. After very little time, I was fairly sure this man did not meet my pillars after all, and he was driving three hours back home by four p.m. that day.

My point here, ladies, is that while we need to listen to our first impressions, we can't let them cloud our judgment. If a man shows serious red flags right off the bat, cut him. But if you see potential, give him a chance, and whether he surprises you in a good way or a bad way, don't be afraid to admit to yourself that you were wrong. Don't stick with the wrong man just because he seemed like Mr. Right at first—that's no way to build a respect-based relationship.

YOUR DARK AND DIRTY

I knew a woman whose husband was on the infamous Ashley Madison list that leaked nationwide. Understandably, her marriage was struggling as a result. I mentioned this to a recently divorced man I had invited over for dinner for our fifth date (my kids were with my ex), and he suddenly became eerily quiet. The shift in energy and behavior was so palpable that I had to ask: "Were you on the Ashley Madison list?" Isn't it interesting how one simple question can change everything? He confessed to being on the Ashley Madison list and to having had an affair.

How do you measure someone else's integrity? Integrity (or lack thereof) is always evident in our most difficult times. So, while the discovery that he had cheated in the past was a red flag on its own, I was more interested in the aftermath. How did he handle his failures? How did he handle his divorce? How did he treat his ex-wife during the process? The answers to these questions are where you will see his integrity, and this is where you will be able to decide whether to respect him or not. This is where you will learn whether you are proud to stand beside him or you'd rather nobody ever knew you went out with him. (By the way, if at any time you think you do not want a potential partner to meet someone close to you, it's time to reevaluate.) In asking him questions, I discovered that the affair was no big deal to this man. What was most important to him were the divorce negotiations. It was crystal clear he had not taken the opportunity to discover why he had an affair, what was broken, and how he could own his shit! Boy, bye!

As I've asked people what they feel is key in a successful relationship, the two most common answers have been trust and communication. So how do you know you can trust someone? How do you build trust in a relationship? After many disappointments and instances of broken trust, the pattern I found in my experiences was a lack of integrity. If a man does not have integrity, how can we trust him?

Identifying signs of integrity became easy after I journaled about the patterns I'd been seeing. One prominent pattern that seemed to lead to broken trust was SnapChat, so I started using this as a litmus test. The app comes with a handy feature that shows you which of your contacts also has the app, so if a potential partner had the app, I decided that he needed to be questioned. Why did he want his content to disappear? What did he have to hide? Who was he keeping information from? Here were the patterns I found: Men who were in relationships and had wandering eyes used this app, and men who chose to send explicit pictures without consent used this app. Neither of these behaviors exhibited integrity, and SnapChat app became a huge red flag in my dating life!

Transparency is another big indicator of integrity. I spend a lot of time researching men online prior to meeting them, and I don't always tell them everything I've learned. I want to give them an opportunity to show me how transparent they're willing to be about their pasts, whether that involves divorce or criminal history or anything else. When you live in a small town, like I do, where there is only one degree of separation between you and anyone you meet, simple questions and conversations with your friends and acquaintances will reveal how open and transparent a potential partner has been. The question is, is this man willing to tell you about his dark and dirty before you find out from somebody else? What type of man do you desire? The one who omits the truth about cheating on his wife until you ask point blank, or the man who is open about how he could have been a better husband in his marriage? When you're evaluating whether a potential partner is a man of integrity, consider how open he is in conversation compared to how transparent you expect him to be.

It was my first Christmas season in the Singlehood, and I had been invited to a holiday party. There was a couple there who was well known in town, and they are both very pretty people. But the husband seemed to follow me from room-to-room all night, and when he finally found the opportunity to have a quiet conversation with me, he propositioned me. He told me that he and his beautiful, successful wife had an agreement to seek the company of others when they each desired, and I had evidently become what he wanted for Christmas that year. Did I mention that I graduated from high school with this couple's children? Whether he really had that agreement with his wife or not, I'll never know. But even if his arrangement had been my cup of tea, his secrecy around the whole thing was a red flag. His values—likely including his integrity—were out of alignment with mine, so I politely refused.

It's not just our potential partners' dark and dirty that we have to deal with—it's our own. How we handle our own mistakes and shortcomings says a lot about our integrity, and the more we can grow in that area, the more we'll attract the men of integrity we're looking for. It takes big faith and courage to work on ourselves, but in order to make breakthroughs when we get "stuck," we must step into the fear that is holding us back. We grow most when we are uncomfortable and we lean into it, and not having a partner to support us during this growth is not easy. But you and I and every other PowerWoman out there is doing the hard work, and we deserve men who are doing the hard work too! As we ladies work on becoming our best selves, we have to hold men accountable for working on themselves too. Maybe they've made mistakes in the past—who hasn't?—but if they're focused on growing and building their integrity, that says a lot too. Here's a test: a great question to ask a man is, "What is the one question you don't want me to ask you?" His answer (or lack of answer) will give you valuable insight into where he needs to grow, where he views his weakness to be, and whether he's even willing to consider that he might need to work on himself. How vulnerable and open will he choose to be with you?

One of my favorite couples has "Truth Sunday" every week. Each Sunday they set aside one solid hour, set a timer, and write questions they want the other to answer with extreme truth. They put the questions in a bowl, sit across from each other, and answer the questions with 100% honestly. This is a great way to practice integrity with one another and build trust in the relationship. What if we all did this when we first started dating someone? What if we set this precedent in the beginning of our relationships? What if we built our relationships on truth and honesty and then maintained that foundation as intentionally as this couple does?

We all have dark and dirty secrets we carry around. How we choose to work through them determines how we show up in the world and how productive we will be. Has your potential partner displayed integrity during his opportunities for growth, and is he vulnerable enough to be transparent with you and earn your trust?

How do you identify integrity in a potential partner?
What questions are you asking to see if someone has
learned from his failures?

How do you hold your partners accountable
for their growth?
What makes you decide to trust a man?

JESUS, TAKE THE WHEEL

When I listed and prioritized the top ten personal values I wanted men to align with, faith was most important to me. Now, before you get all huffy about bringing church into this, let me stop and clarify that, at least the way I see it, there is a very big difference between faith and religion. Religion is church. Faith, on the other hand, is personal.

Regardless of your beliefs, remember that countries have been founded on faith and wars fought over it. Not to mention the number of divorces that misalignment in faith have caused. Chances are, you might want to sync up with your partner in this arena.

So what does faith look like in a relationship? Well, that's different for every couple, based on their specific beliefs. Maybe you both follow Catholic doctrine to a tee, or maybe you both believe in Karma. I have a friend who is in her seventies and has been single for over forty years, and I think she puts it best: "I really want someone to sit in the pew with me." She has a clear, simple picture of what this looks like to her.

It doesn't matter (to me, at least) exactly what pew you're sitting in—what's important is that you're sitting together. I told you that one of my grandmothers dated a man for fifty-four years. One of the biggest reasons they didn't get married before he passed away was that they held different religious beliefs. Faith, religion, and church are frequent topics of conversation where I live, and the older generation in particular is known for having strong opinions. For my grandmother, those opinions were enough to prevent a marriage. But it's not just the older generation that values shared faith. In 2014, the Pew Research Center reported that 44% of adults considered aligning religious beliefs to be "very important" for a successful marriage.[18]

The big question is, do you and the person you're dating see things the same way? That picture of a woman and a man in the pew at church, praying together with his arm around her, is one that many hold onto and continue to search for. Others just want to know you will attend church with them on Christmas and Easter. And others have no interest in religion at all. In her TED Talk about data-driven dating, Amy Webb shared a clear standard in this area:

> "I wanted somebody who was Jew...ish. So I was looking for somebody who had the same background and thoughts on our culture, but wasn't going to force me to go to shul every Friday and Saturday."[19]

For me, it's important that a man has a clearly defined faith in a higher power. If I ask a prospect where he is on his faith journey and his first response is, "I don't believe in organized religion," he's not the one for me. I believe faith brings humility and direction into somebody's life, and I believe that a partner needs to find his own clarity in order to support me in my faith journey. In order for a partner to really understand me and see me, he must understand my faith. In order for a man to affirm me through my faith, his faith must be congruent with mine. Connecting through faith introduces another level of intimacy, and it builds a strong foundation. You may feel differently, and that's ok. It doesn't matter to me what you believe, but it should matter to *you*, and it's important that you make it clear, based on your beliefs, what kind of spiritual life you're looking for in a partner.

I had been in the Singlehood for about two weeks, and I was beginning to think about dating. I called up a good-looking, single guy I'd known for years. We were friends, and I had given him and his family real estate advice a few times, but I hadn't spoken to him in at least six months. He was shocked to learn I was now single, and I was equally shocked to learn he was getting married in two weeks. This was not how the scenario had played out in my head. Still, I respected this man quite a bit, so I took the opportunity to ask him for advice about my new stage in the journey. He gave me the best advice I have ever received about the Singlehood: "Whatever you do, stay strong in your faith."

It's just like I tell my children: your faith is the only thing that will always be with you. We often become discouraged and lonely in the Singlehood, but if we stay strong in our faith, we will find continual encouragement and hope to lift us up. When we connect with somebody through faith, the connection can become so deep it will sustain a relationship despite any and all obstacles, pitfalls, or distractions.

Here's an example of a time I discovered a potential partner and I were misaligned in our faith. It was such a disappointing situation that I really needed that encouragement and hope. I used to travel to Austin, Texas, sometimes for business. On one trip, I met a man who had been a pastor on Benny Hinn's team. (Don't worry, I didn't know who that was either. Thank the lord for Mother Google! Benny Hinn was a televangelist and crusader along the lines of Billy Graham, and Hinn had his own fall from grace.) This man was smooth, he was fun, and every time I was in town, he would take me to dinner. The groceries were good, but I hoped and believed this one might be worth more than just the dinners. He was entering a new career, and we had fun together. He quoted scripture to me and affirmed me through my faith. It seemed as though we were aligned on some of my most important pillars.

Then one night I was on the phone with him, and he was discussing a sermon with me. Suddenly, everything about him changed, and you could hear it through the phone. He was a different person. He'd led me to believe that he'd put crusading behind him in favor of a more authentic religious life, but it was like the ghost of Benny Hinn's Christmas Past had come to visit. The stereotypical televangelist voice, banter, and call for donations came alive on that phone call! Nope. Done. Next! It is disappointing to discover anyone's been inauthentic, much less a pastor. But it all became clear that the dude was literally putting on a show. It turned out he was trying to go back into TV evangelism after all, and he'd been playing on my faith in order to steer the journey his way. But, darlin', I did not see myself as the next Tammy Faye Bakker. (Of course, the other takeaway from this experience, and the one I probably should have seen right away, is that you should be very wary of men "of the cloth" who are hanging out on dating apps. I mean, I'm not real sure how I would feel about seeing my pastor on a dating app. Are you?)

Be careful when you're assessing whether you and a potential partner are aligned in faith, because, unfortunately, there are men who will play a role they don't really believe in just to get in your good graces. Someone's "advertised" faith may be very different from his true practices or beliefs. And it's not just allegedly reformed televangelists you have to watch out for. Several friends have suggested that I join a singles group at church. But, interestingly enough, I know of too many single guys who have joined singles groups at church to troll for women, with no intention of practicing their faith. So, I'm skeptical. And besides, when I go to church, I am focused on my spiritual growth, not my dating life or my business or anything else. My time with my faith is very focused.

So when you start dating someone new, when do you bring up the conversation of faith? When do you start to assess whether you're aligned, not only in your faith but also in the value you place on faith? It's easy to dismiss this conversation early on, only to discover that a misalignment in faith is causing problems as the relationship deepens. Worst case, you get married and have children before it becomes an issue! I have found that having this conversation even before a first date is beneficial for me, because my faith is such an important part of my life. Darlin', I am busy, and I do not have time to waste. If you do not meet my standards, I do not have time for dinner—or anything else, frankly.

Now, this conversation should never be degrading or judgmental but open minded and enlightening. As in all things, it's important to come from curiosity. The point isn't to prove someone else wrong but to understand where they are coming from and whether they're headed in the same direction as you. Spiritual beliefs are usually a good indicator of whether you're on the same overall path.

When you close your eyes, what do you envision your spiritual life with your partner will look like? Do you need his arm around you in the pew?

If he wants you to attend church, will that be an issue
for you?
Is it important to you to marry somebody within your faith?

I don't know what your top ten values are, and that's okay. They may look nothing like mine, and that's okay too. What I do know for sure is that there are no accidents, and we are all placed in each other's paths for a purpose. When we see people in our paths whose values do not align with ours, those encounters are meant to reaffirm us in our journeys, teaching us to hold firm to our values and maintain the standards that are important to each of us. These people help us gain clarity around the path we want to choose. So pay close attention, and don't let your standards slip. They will define the years you might spend with somebody.

In Love with Being in Love

Stereotypically, women are often seen as hopeless romantics while men date strictly for sex. In one study, though, 63% of college-aged men and 83% of college-aged women said they preferred a traditional romantic relationship to an uncommitted sexual relationship.[20] Yes, more women than men were looking for relationships, but the majority of both sexes were looking for more than just sex. The takeaway is this: at some point, the majority of us are in love with the idea of being in love.

As I reflect, I see that when I entered the Singlehood, I was very much in love with being in love. "Infatuated" might even be a better term, because my idea of love back then wasn't exactly a model of true, realistic love. My world was broken, and I wanted the fairytale the Pinterest boards portrayed. Unfortunately, all I had found so far were frogs, and I was no princess. When you are in love with being in love, you make choices based on an unrealistic dream, not on reality. Consequently, I made poor choices and found repeated disappointment. I finally realized that I needed to fall out of love with love and fall in love with my life instead. I needed to become more infatuated with my growth, my world, and my future than with the search for a partner.

93

I had become the classic girl in the dating world—the one who is always either in a relationship or seeking a relationship. This girl is in love with being in love instead of with who she is and where she is going. I had become a girl I never wanted to become. Interestingly enough, though, the more dates I went on, the more I was turned off by dating (and by this girl). So, the more alone I was. God was forcing me to be alone, which was right where I needed to be.

I needed to discover more of myself, what I enjoyed, where I found joy, and whom I enjoyed being around, and I needed to dance in my underwear more often. Once I started working on myself, the perspective I gained was amazing. Letting go of this dream, this expectation, was so liberating. I had to learn to become comfortable being alone in order to learn to love the life I had—the life without a partner. Many of us in the Singlehood feel isolated and alone. But the reality is, you are not alone. We all experience this season, and you will rise above it as well.

THE LONELY

Everyone's journey into and through the Singlehood is different. Each woman's story has its tragedy and drama, its shock and awe, and, in the end, its victory, right? My journey—and your journey too—is just that: a journey. It is ever-changing, ever-evolving, and different from everyone else's.

But no matter how we wound up single, all of us PowerWomen have one thing in common: we all know the Lonely. What is the Lonely? It's the moments in the Singlehood that we do not post on social media. It's the parts we don't dream about when we're in bad relationships and fantasizing about being single. It's the utterly unromanticized, unglamorous aspects of the Singlehood. We all experience the Lonely in different ways and on different levels, but we all experience it. It's not something we openly discuss at parties over cocktails. It's not something we're prepared for as we enter the Singlehood, because nobody warns us just how hard being single can be, and nobody discusses the Lonely, except maybe on the therapist's couch.

Well, darlin', I say enough with sweeping the Lonely under the rug. We're not doing ourselves or our sisters any good by bottling it up. It's time to talk about it! Because here's the thing about the Lonely: it doesn't discriminate. Whether we're married or single or in a fifty-four-year-long relationship, the Lonely can find us. No matter who we are, we all identify with this feeling at different points in our lives. We all need a tribe to lift us up and help us remember our own self-worth. But how can we find that tribe if we can't talk about the Lonely? Why are we so hesitant to reach out to one another to ask for support or even just to say hello? Why aren't we more generous about reaching out to help others with our time and gifts? What are we so afraid of? What is the worst thing that could happen? More relationships? Is that such a bad thing? How can we expect others to help us through our Lonely if we don't help through theirs?

Have you ever quietly closed your eyes and thought about your greatest fear? When I entered the Singlehood, my greatest fear was that my marital status would prohibit me from being present for my children. Once I realized that I am and always will be present with my children, my greatest fear became being alone the rest of my life. After much research, I realized I shared this fear with most single people—and plenty of married people too! The *Huffington Post* recently published an article about a study on the fear of being alone.[21] Of 153 participants, here's what they found:

- 40% said they feared not having a long-term companion.
- 18% said they feared "spinsterhood."
- 12% feared losing a current partner.
- 11% feared growing old alone.

On some level it was reassuring to know I was normal to feel this way. But the study also found this fear of being alone caused many people to settle for and stay in unhealthy or unsatisfying relationships, lowering their standards in order to have companionship. Do we really struggle with self-worth so much that we'd rather be in toxic relationships than cultivate relationships with ourselves?

I started to question how I was going to empower myself to overcome this fear. To start, I identified all the things that were life-threatening about being alone so that I could really define what I had to be afraid of. I could only come up with two potentially fatal scenarios: First, with no one present to help me do my quarterly mole checks, I may miss an early diagnosis of skin cancer. And second, nobody would be in bed with me to notice if I developed sleep apnea. Then I realized I had doctors who could handle both of those things. So if there was nothing life-threatening about being alone, then where was the Lonely coming from? Upon serious reflection, complete with many difficult conversations with my own reflection in the mirror, I learned that the Lonely wasn't driven by any need for a companion—it was driven by a need to feel loved, valued, and appreciated. And while dating could be a temporary fix, the only way to cure the Lonely for good was to learn to love, value, and appreciate myself. The biggest question I had to ask myself was, how will anyone else see and appreciate my light, joy, and goodness if I don't see it for myself? What I would learn was, the more I loved myself, my world, and those who surrounded me, the quieter the Lonely would become.

But I hadn't learned that quite yet, and then, the Lonely was palpable. I had defined myself as "wife" for my entire adult life, and now I no longer knew who I was. My bed was empty for the first time in fourteen years, and I was single for the first time since age 17. When you are married, you become accustomed to having someone there to share guidance about major decisions, help with the children, laugh with you, and give you a hug at the end of the day. Sometimes, even just knowing there's another body present is a huge comfort. But that stability was gone, and now I was relying solely on myself—something I had never learned how to do. At 34-years-old, I had never even paid bills myself. I hadn't slept alone in a home more than a handful of times in my life. Now that I was single and sharing custody of my kids, many evenings the only sound in the house was my own internal monologue, which was scary. And many mornings, in the absence of the bustle I was so accustomed to, I found myself talking to myself to ward off the deafening new silence. I no longer had a partner to help me along this journey, and my closest friends were all married. None of them could really relate to what I was experiencing. I was, for the first time, alone. This was a new level of growth. The fear of the unknown was overwhelming. I was reframing my role as sole provider for myself and my children, and the pressure was immense.

I started to find new hobbies and new friends and became comfortable talking to myself all the time, and the Lonely started to ease up for a while. But then the holidays came. The holidays are always the most interesting time for the Lonely. It's strong, from Thanksgiving to New Year's Day, because those days are all about love and togetherness, and when it seems like everyone around us is partnered up—and when, between the Hallmark Channel lineup and Netflix's *Christmas Prince* obsession, we can't get away from picture-perfect on-screen romance—we feel as though we're constantly being reminded that we're on our own. So the winter months tend to be the most difficult and vulnerable. And, conveniently enough, they're also the months when the boys will start coming out of the woodwork. It seems they're feeling the Lonely too, because as the holidays get closer, the number of invitations and texts a single girl receives grows exponentially. The peak is New Year's Day, when we all tend to evaluate where we have been and where we are headed for the upcoming year. I always keep a running tally with my other single girlfriends to see who has the most "Happy New Year" texts from dudes. They're feeling the Lonely too, but tread lightly, and always pay attention to their patterns! That combination of holiday-inspired vulnerability and higher-than-usual availability of attention can be lethal, encouraging us to forget our standards and dive into something that's bound to end in heartbreak.

New Year's Day or not, we all experience painful events that shape our paths and usher in the Lonely. But those painful events—and the Lonely they bring—will trigger some of our largest growth opportunities if we let them. The Lonely is where I have discovered who I am, how I function, where my release is, and why I matter! We all need the Lonely at some point in our lives, and some of us need more than others, depending on how much growing we have to do. The Lonely is necessary, so embrace it, lean into it, and be thankful for it. But find a balance, because we cannot stay in the Lonely for long.

The key to getting out of the Lonely is to never allow it to lower your standards—for yourself or your mate. Every time someone who is unhappily married asks me about dating and the Singlehood, I immediately encourage them to work on the set of issues they are currently struggling with. Remember my daddy's warning against trading in one set of issues for another? This is where that advice rings so, so true. A married couple may be able to overcome the Lonely together if they're both willing to put in the work. If they actively try and they're still not a good match, well, all the growing they've done will mean they take less of the Lonely with them into the Singlehood. But if they give up on their marriage—whether they settle into the unhappiness or throw in the towel before trying to grow—then they'll be settling into a whole lot of Lonely. The Lonely is always among us, and it can make you wonder if anyone will ever come along and see you, accept you, and love you for all you are and all you have to offer. But even when the Lonely is deep, you have to refuse to settle.

Once you learn how to be independent and confident and find happiness in yourself, the Lonely will lift. It won't be gone forever—it'll come back now and then, when you least expect it. But when it does, you'll find it's easier to climb back out of than it was before. Once you can be alone without feeling the Lonely, you'll begin to embrace your alone time and value it for your own self-care. This confidence and independence make it easier to say "Thank you, next," or "I'm sober now, and you need to go home." When you no longer fear the Lonely, you will be more selective about who occupies space with you.

LESSONS OF A SINGLE MOM

When one is in single parenthood, the Lonely is more than the loss of a partner, it is the loss of a dream we created, and many times we date too soon in an attempt to quiet the Lonely. But to really climb out of the Lonely, we must create a new dream and a new story, allowing joy to come into our world.

When I divòrced, my biggest loss was that I no longer had my kids 100% of the time. The days without packing school lunches, driving carpool duty, or smelling sweaty kids were my greatest fear becoming reality. Sleep didn't come easy, because when I closed my eyes, I saw the smiles of my children and heard the sweetness of their voices. Filling my time with positive activities and people became the only way to find joy in the midst of my hell.

But what if we could reframe the Lonely as a gift? As parents, we pour into our children at a high level, and we forget to give ourselves time to reset and rest. Our time without our children invites in the Lonely, but it also provides a space for us to learn about ourselves again and to enjoy things we haven't been able to participate in while we were taking care of our children.

In order to discover what brings you joy now, leverage the Lonely. Use that time to discover new activities, hobbies, and friendships. You will feel more whole in your new joy, the Lonely will eventually dissipate, and your children will feel it too.

When have you felt the Lonely?
What has shaped who you are?
What hobbies have you always wanted to experience?
How are you being purposeful in creating new friendships?
What activities can you now attend that will help you grow?
Who do you want to become, and what do you
need to do to get there?
How are you finding gratitude in the Lonely
in order to overcome your fears?

DON'T FALL FOR THE HYPE

If you're finding yourself falling hard into the Lonely or infatuated with the idea of being in love, it's no wonder! Everywhere we turn these days, society and the media are reinforcing the idea that being married is far preferable to being single and that being in a relationship is the most important thing we can achieve.

Turn on the TV, and you'll find shows built around finding a relationship in thirty days, choosing the perfect wedding dress (by committee, I might add), planning the perfect wedding, and watching other people plan theirs. There are magazines and websites and apps to help you plan your big day, and there's an extremely profitable industry around weddings. (Not so much the marriages, themselves, of course.) Are we in love with the hype of being in love? Are we projecting that on to our youth? Is this the message of women's empowerment our sisters had in mind when they fought for our freedoms?

Here's the truth, ladies: despite what the media might tell you, women today are less focused on our wedding days and more focused on our career goals and dreams. Women are waiting to marry until much later, giving second thoughts to having children, and even empowering themselves to enter parenthood in nontraditional ways. So why do we give our attention and money to media that portrays such an antiquated picture? *The Bachelor, The Bachelorette, The Proposal, 90 Day Fiancé,* and *Married at First Sight* really underestimate women! What if there were TV shows about women getting CEO positions rather than getting engaged? What if a romantic comedy portrayed a woman falling in love with herself, her life, and her own growth? Wouldn't that give our daughters a new perspective? Why in the fresh hell has the media not turned its attention to the modern woman's dreams? Those may include rings and dresses, sure, but there's so much more that we want—and so much more we're willing to spend our money on!

And speaking of money, Business Insider reports that the average cost of a wedding in the United States is $38,700.[22] Now, consider the cost of a wedding as an investment, and then consider the divorce rate. That wedding is a pretty risky investment, isn't it? If the ideal return on our wedding investment is a happy, lifelong relationship, then why aren't we investing that much into the relationships themselves before we tie the knot? What if the parents who pay for their children's weddings invested that much in relationship coaching to ensure their children had happy, healthy relationships for many years to come? What do our investment choices teach our children? Is a big party more important than their relationships? Darlin', don't get me wrong: I love a good wedding. But a wedding is just a single day, and the reality is, you're planning for your partner to be with you forever. He may be dressed in a tux, clean-shaven, smelling good, and on his best behavior on your wedding day, but how often will you see that version of your man? Likewise, how often will he see you in a four-thousand-dollar dress with professionally done hair and makeup? Most days, he'll be biting his nails, picking his nose, or snoring—and you will too—so you'd better be okay with that!

It's not just traditional media and the wedding industry that perpetuate the hype. Social media is equally complicit, and what's worse is that social media makes it personal. (If you're not on social media, more power to you, and feel free to skip the rest of this section! But if you are, listen up!) We see our friends' photos with their new boyfriends, their shiny new diamonds, and their perfectly coiffed bridesmaids, and we wonder when it will be our turn. There are certain times of the year when engagements peak—typically the infamous holiday season—and social media becomes nauseating to those in the Singlehood. We eat up the hype, but it can quickly propel us into the Lonely. And that Lonely can tempt us to perpetuate the hype too, posting selfies with every new boy we go out with, changing our relationship statuses, posting sappy tributes to the boys we like...all in the name of making it look like we're living our best romantic lives.

Darlin, here's the skinny: social media is for your life, and your life is so much more than a relationship. So instead of hyping your dating life, why not hype your life? Share photos of what really fulfills you—your friends, your career, your solo adventures—and three things will happen: first, you'll stop being victim to the hype and you'll feel the Lonely ease up. Second, you'll be helping out your single sisters by encouraging them to celebrate their own self-worth separate from their relationships. Third, you'll start to attract more men of quality through your social media presence, because it's not just other women who are studying your profile. Boys are absolutely looking at your social media too. They may not comment, but they're there and sometimes they'll accidentally let it slip. I'll see a male colleague in the field, and he'll say something like, "Hey, saw you went skiing..." He certainly isn't on my Christmas letter list, so how does he know? He's been social media stalking me. Here's another way I can tell: since I use social media primarily for business, the phone number I publish on my accounts is a Google Voice number my whole team uses to stay better connected to our clients. So when boys text me at that number, I know they found it by stalking my social media, and it makes the next day's team meeting extra fun! Remember, you attract what you are, and that's true online too. If you want to attract someone who appreciates all that you are—and who is a candidate for a long-term relationship—then celebrate *all* that you are, and not just your relationship status, on social media.

One of my villagers told me in the very beginning of my dating life, "You must stay mysterious." How else will you pique their interest? So until you have a ring on your finger, do not post photos with your dates. And there is absolutely no reason to list a relationship status on social media. When you're single, you don't need to broadcast it. If a man of quality is into you, he will seek you out and ask. And even then, remain mysterious. After all, imagine you've posted umpteen pictures of you and your brandnew fling, and then you break up. How are you going to go tell the world you're single again? A break-up announcement post is never pretty, but you won't need to post one if you never posted about that boy to begin with! Do yourself—and the rest of us in the Singlehood—a favor and stop playing into the hype on social media. When you do, you'll feel the Lonely giving way to your own sense of confidence and worth.

IS BEING ALONE SUCH A BAD THING?

Too often, when we try to discuss our fears with others, we are told to "put on our big girl panties." Well, my "big girl panties" lost their elastic years ago, and it's more fun to go commando anyway! So let's talk about those fears, because so much of the Lonely comes from the many different fears we all carry around. For some of us, the biggest fear is that we've become permanent residents of the Singlehood. We think, "Am I making a career of singlehood?" "Is this my new normal?" But that begs the question, "Is the Singlehood really such a bad place to be for a while?" You've already proven you can do everything on your own, so why do you fear doing tomorrow alone?

Remember what most of us were taught as little girls? That we are to grow up, get married, have babies, and die. Everything centers around our relationships with others—daughter, wife, mother—and our ability to procreate. We are not groomed to think we can do life alone; we are taught that our identities are dependent on someone else. This programming is a big part of what causes the Lonely. Yes, it is wonderful to have a partner for life's events. Yes, it is wonderful to have someone by your side to celebrate you and support you. But is it necessary? No, ma'am! It is time to change this mindset and empower ourselves. We *can* do life on our own, and we *will* do life on our own. If there is someone worthy of our attention, then that's great and we can make time, but there is no reason we need a man to have a fulfilling and successful life. It is time we model an independent life for our children too, so they can gain the confidence in knowing that they can succeed alone and that they'll never feel they need to settle for the wrong partner just because he or she is there.

This fear of the Lonely can cause us to remarry immediately upon entering the Singlehood, making another mistake and winding up right back on Tinder. Hello, rebound dude! It's not surprising that studies show 90% of rebound relationships fail, and most of them only last two months or less. In other words, the first guy we meet after entering the Singlehood is not the right guy to leave it with. When we rebound, we're usually trying to avoid our fears by attaching them to someone else, and this isn't fair to either party: it builds a false foundation and ultimately leads to disappointment. Here's a rebound story a girlfriend of mine lived after a three-year divorce: The divorce process had been even more painful than the Lonely. She was a runner and very athletic with an amazing body. Did I mention she was also a physician and extremely accomplished? The whole package, right there, and she was finally single again. Then she showed up to book club one day and told us all about this guy she'd met. He was a DJ, which was cool and exciting! He lived an hour away, which was not ideal, but she was thrilled, so we could get onboard. But then she told us he went by the stage name "DJ Snaggletooth," and none of us could get behind that. Consistent with the studies, this rebound relationship was short-lived, thank goodness. This woman is brilliant, and she knew her value proposition—and her standards for men definitely included a full set of teeth!

On the other hand, fear can also cause us to pass on people who could be amazing additions to our lives. We resist reaching out to them or learning from them or connecting with them because we fear losing them, too, and falling right back into the Lonely.

As uncomfortable as the Lonely may be, you will only master your independence when you lean into that discomfort, embrace the idea of building a strong relationship with yourself, and open yourself up to the idea that being alone can be a very good thing. I heard Gary Keller, author of *The One Thing*, speak at a conference, and this amazing quote has stuck with me ever since: "Mastery is found when you do that which is uncomfortable so often it becomes uncomfortable to not do it." Being alone in a quiet house was extremely uncomfortable when I entered the Singlehood. But in order to master the Singlehood and self-care, we have to become okay with alone time, even looking forward to it and using it as an opportunity to learn more about who we are and how we can best take care of ourselves. After four years in the Singlehood, I find myself grateful for the nights I am alone, with no work appointments and no plans other than to workout, go home, and take a nice hot bath in silence. If you do not have this time to discover yourself, then how will someone else be able to see your value and meet your needs?

It's okay to be alone. Don't rush to find your next partner because you think you're supposed to or because you think you can't do it on your own. Take control of your scenario, your life, and your power. We must all have our own identities, our own hobbies, and activities we enjoy on our own. Then, we can share those things with another. In other words, we are much more than wife, husband, mother, father, child, or friend. We are our own unique selves, and that is something we should all appreciate. But sometimes, it takes being alone—for a night or a week or a month or a year or more—to really learn how to embrace ourselves. Your greatness and potential are waiting to be uncovered, and everyone around you will bathe in your light as you allow it to shine! Do not let the fear paralyze you. Instead, let yourself blossom!

PAIN INTO PLEASURE

One big key to combatting the Lonely is to find gratitude for everything and everyone. This will keep you focused, positive, purposeful, and passionate! Even when you are feeling lonely, gratitude will help you maintain growth and independence and stay focused on what is most important. If I hadn't been forced into the Lonely, I would have never discovered my passions for helping and growing others, journaling, reading, or yoga.

Many people who are new to the Singlehood or deep in the Lonely wonder how one can find gratitude in these circumstances. For me, at least, it wasn't easy. I had to lose what I thought was most important in my life to truly see and understand how much I had to be grateful for. Prior to the divorce, I found myself always wanting more and never satisfied with what was around me. Since then, I have learned to meet myself where I am, in gratitude for the many blessings in my life, rather than chasing what I don't have. Find your gratitude, and you'll start to feel the positivity flowing through you. Focus on the good, and the good will expand. Because you, my dear, are full of goodness!

One thing in particular that we need to be grateful for, especially when we're in the Singlehood—are our friendships. It can be easy to get so bogged down in the search for a partner that we brush off old friends or pass up opportunities to make new ones. But when we're in the Singlehood, we need our tribes more than ever. I have even made some amazing friendships from dating apps. I met one in particular on my 36th birthday. He was—and still is—one of the hottest guys I have ever met. Picture a Ralph Lauren cover model, aged 45, from New England, and that's this guy! Hello! Jesus loves me! He was extremely intelligent and had extreme depth, which made him even hotter! (If there's one thing I can't do, it's stupid.) We'd been chatting for several weeks, and he finally asked me out on my birthday, though he didn't know it was my birthday until later. We met for drinks after my birthday dinner with close friends. The conversation was great, he was into me, and he asked me to come back to his place. I politely declined. Like a gentleman, he held my hand and walked me to my car without any trace of disappointment. But when we got there, he started making out with me against my car. His hand started to go up my skirt, and all I could think was *"We are literally in the middle of the street."* I stopped him and said goodbye. He was a good one. I wanted this one. He had never been married and didn't have children. He had a great career he was passionate about, and he loved his family deeply. He was a good guy! But it wasn't going to work out for us romantically, because he worked in my town half of the week and in another state the other half of the week, and he was clear that he wanted to go back to New England to be close to family.

It would have been easy to take the all-or-nothing approach, so laser-focused on finding a partner that, if he wasn't the right fit, I would cut him out of my life. It would've been even easier to go back to his place that night and tell myself I'd just deal with the fallout later. But I knew we needed each other platonically during that season, and we respected one another deeply. I chose to be grateful for this wonderful man who'd come into my life even if it wasn't in the way I'd hoped for. Even though we couldn't be partners, we became good friends, and we saw each other every week when he was in town. Sometimes, we need one another in the Singlehood to help with the Lonely. Finding these friendships and remembering to be grateful for the incredible relationships we have will help us battle the Lonely and keep us from jumping into bad relationships.

What are you grateful for?
What nonromantic relationships do you lean on
to combat the Lonely?
Have you inadvertently neglected your tribe in
your effort to find a partner?
How are you reframing relationships with men to
serve you best in your season?

If you are like me, you avoid the Lonely as much as possible. But inevitably, life's uninvited events bring it right back despite our best efforts, and we are forced to grieve our loss. That's uncomfortable, but it's good and necessary. If we do not process our pain, then we can't open ourselves to the pleasure that's to come. The independence and confidence you can achieve when you lean into the Lonely will sustain you. And remember, while you may envy others' relationships, there will always be someone envying your circumstances too. It is too easy to bathe in our victimhood and overlook everything we have to be grateful for. The strongest, most fulfilling choice you can make is to rise and find the joy!

How are you choosing to rise?
How are you choosing to focus on the joy?

The Wet Factor

I was a year into the dating pool when I joined some colleagues at a piano bar after our company Christmas party.
I was kid-free that night, or so I thought, so I went out! A
group of boys—yes, boys—kept eyeing us until, finally, one
of them approached and started to chat me up. I knew he
was young, but he had a beard, and I love a beard. Besides,
I needed to know just how much groove I had left! So I let
the small talk progress: Where are you from? What do you
do? Then, I asked his age: 27. *Damn*, I thought, *I'm doing
pretty good!*

The boy said he and his group were in town celebrating
a friend's college graduation. Then he said he was a pharmaceutical rep. It is always, always beneficial to be the sober
woman interviewing the drunk dude! You catch all the
inconsistencies. For example, why is a 27-year-old pharmaceutical rep on a trip with a group of college kids and fresh
grads? So, I asked when he had graduated. One question was
all it took for him to crack! He admitted he wasn't a pharmaceutical rep; in fact, he was still in college. I asked him
what his real age was, and he gave it up real easy. He was 21!
I wanted to see a driver's license, and when he pulled it out
I saw it was the special license for underage drivers. He was

so freshly 21 that he hadn't even made it to the DMV to get the big-kid license!

"Honey," I said, "you are jailbait!" He gave me the same look my son gives me. You know, the one that says, "I'm sorry, I just lost my puppy, but please anyway?" That night, I learned another reason to not date someone from an after-hours venue: you might become an accidental pedophile!

Speaking of young love, do you remember the last time you fell head over heels? Did you get butterflies in your stomach every time you looked at your man, or even thought about him? Makes you feel like a teenager again (or a bright-green 21-year-old), doesn't it? But guess what? Those butterflies are good! If just thinking about your man in the beginning of the relationship *doesn't* give you butterflies, then you have to cut him, because this is an actual stage of love—the first stage, in fact—and Dorothy Tennov named it "limerence" in 1979.[23] This is the phase where you have sweaty palms, butterflies in your stomach, and raging hormones. In this phase, you think constantly about the next time you will just talk to each other—not to mention spend time together! Based on all my reading, this phase can last from two months to two years, but in a strong relationship, the underlying desire should not fade even when the butterflies slow down.

Down the road a ways, there will come a time when you've settled into your relationship, and he'll do something that will make you so mad at him you will want to literally "cut him" (but you won't because that would definitely go against this dating pillar—and probably several others). But because you're in a strong, lasting, sustainable relationship, you'll look across the kitchen table at this man who has made you so damned angry, and you'll think to yourself, *"Dammit, he's so hot!"* You'll still want to clear the table, crawl across it, and take advantage of him even though you are furious! This is why this pillar is so crucial. Initiating the wet factor is one thing, but maintaining it requires a level of intimacy that will sustain some of the valleys in a relationship. Long after the butterflies are gone, the wet factor helps us remember not only *that* we love our partners but *why* we love them, even when we're furious. And when we remember those things, we're better equipped to solve our problems constructively rather than letting them fester or sweeping them under the rug where they'll turn into resentment. So good news, ladies: keeping your relationship hot actually makes it more sustainable! And besides, what man doesn't love a table crawl?

I call it the "wet factor," because...well, you get it, don't you? And it does begin with physical attraction, but we women know it's much more than that. It has to be, because, frankly, ain't nobody going to look the same when they're 80! Maybe it's his brain that turns you on, or his sense of humor, or his compassion, or his romantic streak. Discern what is important to you in this pillar—what's your own personal "wet factor?" I have girlfriends who have cut men who have fulfilled all the other pillars simply because they were bad kissers. And I support that! You have ask yourself, "What am I willing to live with for as long as we both shall live?" These women weren't willing to live with mediocre kissing, and they weren't willing to lower their standards either.

Sometimes, identifying the wet factor—and then making the connection when you find it—requires a little negotiation. It did the first time I experienced it, for sure, and coming from the business world, there is nothing I love more than negotiations!

I matched with a man who was in town on a road trip with his brother, and he asked me to dinner. Keeping it social, I invited a single girlfriend along to accompany my date's brother. As soon as we arrived, it became completely clear to me that my girlfriend and I were going to have to switch dates. They were both good looking men and successful, fun, and intelligent. However, I could not ignore my attraction to the brother. When our food arrived and he prayed over our meal, that attraction went through the roof. Sweet Mary, mother of Joseph, this was a man of faith! Did I mention he was also a model in California? This was the first time I'd ever felt the urge to crawl across the table, and I didn't care that it was a public place.

It was time to focus on negotiations and make the switch! I started texting my girlfriend from across the dinner table, and she wanted to switch as much as I did! Now, all I had to do was be patient and wait on the perfect timing in order to lean into the motivation. The man I had originally matched with was recently divorced, and it was clear he was looking for approval, affection, and attention from a woman. So, when an opportunity presented itself, I explained how much my girlfriend was into him—showcasing *her*, not *me* as the woman who could give him that approval tonight—and we made the switch. Never underestimate a woman who knows what she wants and understands the power of negotiations! The wet factor is real, and sometimes we have to work for it, but it will always be worth it.

When we're in the Singlehood with high standards like these, getting laid on a regular basis becomes a problem—a first-world problem, sure, but still a problem. Days become months, and months become years. (Well, for some people.) There have been times in my life when I didn't know if I would ever know what intimacy was again. Of course, there's a difference between true intimacy and sex, and I'll have more to share on that later on in this chapter. But I had never heard of a "sexual peak" until I entered the Singlehood in my mid-30s. You can imagine my disappointment when I read the *Women's Health* article that said a woman's peak was around the age of 30, and I discovered I'd missed my chance.[24] What kind of sick joke was this? Not only had I been thrown into the Singlehood, but I had been thrown into it *after* my sexual peak? Fortunately, rather than throwing in the towel right then and there, I kept reading. It turns out the researchers had found that most people believed they were having the best sex of their lives at their current age, no matter how old they were. Evidently, we are all just grateful to be having sex at all, and it makes us feel as if we are in our prime!

So if you're worried about your sexual peak, there's still hope. But still, maintaining a certain standard as a single PowerWoman is tough, especially when we're newly single. We miss feeling desired or wanted and being physically touched. But when a woman realizes her value proposition, she also realizes just how hot she really is. This confidence makes it easier to maintain her standards and helps her hold back until she finds somebody who truly deserves the goods. It's not easy at first, and it can be tempting to "give it up" for boys who don't deserve it just because they make us feel wanted, but those boys haven't earned the privilege yet. There comes a point when a woman knows what she desires in a partner, loves her whole self, and is willing to hold on until she feels confident in giving herself to someone who meets her standards—and satisfies her "wet factor."

Do not lose hope! Find your joy, and bathe in it! Love, intimacy, and an undying "wet factor" will come!

*When you imagine yourself at age 80, what is most
important in a relationship?
What are your standards for a man who satisfies this pillar?
What makes you look forward to talking with him, sharing
with him, going through life with him?
What makes you want to crawl across the table
even when you're angry?*

LESSONS OF A SINGLE MOM

As mothers in the Singlehood, many of us compare ourselves to the hot single women who have never birthed children, are free of stretchmarks or FUPAs (fat upper pussy areas), and have pretty, perky breasts. Do not fear: she too will become old and wrinkled, and gravity will ravage her body as well. Many of us have allowed only the fathers of our children to see the fried eggs on our chests—also known as our post-breastfeeding boobs—and we fear that we will no longer be attractive to men because we are no longer young. What I have learned through many conversations with men is that the right one will love and desire all of you, including your imperfections. And, according to one male dating coach and the men he's surveyed, the single mom who has her shit together is even more attractive than the single woman without kids.[25] The single PowerMom has proven she can love, nurture, succeed in both business and relationships, and juggle all the crystal balls. Likewise, successful men find our breed extremely attractive, including our childbearing bodies.

D-SQUARED: THE HOOKUP STAGE

Remember how I promised there'd be more on sex (as opposed to intimacy) later in this chapter? Well, immediately after my divorce was final, the girls from the office decided to take me out to a club because 1) my divorce was final and 2) I had lived an extremely sheltered life and had never been to a club before. Literally, never. Yes, I went to college, yes, I was 34-years-old, and no, I had never been to a club—at least, not the kind with a DJ and booze and scantily clad people looking to hook up. I know you're reading this in disbelief. But remember, I was still in college when I got married at age 20 and started my career at age 21, and we started trying to have kids soon after that. I attribute so much of my wonderful life to the discipline I have always imposed upon myself, but I was about to live a little!

My coworkers informed me that my wardrobe was too "mommyish," and they decided to dress me—or undress me, if we're being honest—themselves. I think we were all having flashbacks to that scene from *Knocked Up* where the bouncer denies certifiable hotties Kathryn Heigle and Leslie Mann access, saying, "I can't let you in 'cause you're old as fuck." Just imagine a group of moms in their late 30s and 40s at a club in a small town in the South. We did our best. I was freezing my ass off in a denim mini skirt and black halter top, but our group was still the most conservatively dressed people there. We stood out just a bit, but this was the only club we had.

Just when the girls had heard enough of my bitching and finally agreed to let me leave, a man standing nearby asked me to hold his drink like he knew me. I was so surprised—and clueless—that I took it and just stared at him. He rolled up his sleeves, introduced himself, and offered to buy me a drink! I had never had a guy buy me a drink! I'd noticed men noticing me in the past, but I'd always been a married woman, so I'd put on my blinders and refused to notice them back. Even today, I still struggle to discern whether a man is being friendly or flirting.

I was fresh meat in the Singlehood. So much so that, when he asked me what I wanted, I responded with, "alcohol." (I am one of the most social people you will meet, but I am not a drinker. I had never been truly drunk in my life until I was 35-years-old.) He graciously handed me a vodka cranberry. It was terrible. Then he invited me to dinner later that week at a really nice restaurant in town, took my digits, and asked me to go home with him.

The girls freaked out until I told them I had already Googled him in the bathroom. I could find no record of misbehavior from this dude (and I'm a good Googler), so off I went. The girls followed me and texted all night, checking on me. Despite my willingness to live a little, this dude had had so much to drink that there was no way to have sex with him. I had RSVP'd yes to my first girl/boy slumber party at age 34, but sadly (or maybe fortunately), it ended early. To reassure the girls of my safety, I sent them a selfie with me next to the passed-out Mr. Limp Biscuit, and then I went home.

What I learned that night is that you will be able to get some free drinks at the club, and maybe even a decent dinner date, but a vibrator and a bottle of wine are probably a better deal. They'll never disappoint, they'll never talk back, and they'll always get the job done.

So what was I doing, going home with this guy in the first place? Every single woman goes through this phase in her dating life, so let's get real, using some acronyms that have become common in my village: any smart girl can have D-squared (dick and dinner) with an HPA (hot piece of ass) so she can share a DR (dick report) the next day. There have been times when we've said, "That's it! I'm just dating for D-squared, nothing else!" Sometimes, we don't even care about the dinner. And if we are going to get some, it's gonna be with an HPA! And we will always have a DR for our girlfriends the following day. You know it's going to be good when it starts with "You won't believe what this man..."

As I have reflected on my dating history and spoken at length with many women about their dating histories, I've learned, after divorce, that many men and women go through a season of living it up. This looks very different for everyone. I know a woman who never online dated. She logged on to test the waters, relishing in the attention of men online, but she never partook in any dates. I know a conservative church woman whose wild run consisted of dinner with a tattooed, atheist biker. I know a woman who left a marriage having not had an orgasm in years, got online right away, and interviewed men in order to find one who could help her achieve her very specific goal. What all these women have in common is that they've experienced a lack of intimacy for a long period of time—often starting long before they entered the Singlehood—and they are looking to fill the void.

Many times in both marriage and the Singlehood, we get so lonely that we no longer know what physical touch feels like, much less intimacy. I remember getting a pedicure and thinking how wonderful it was to have someone touch me because it had been so long that I no longer remembered how it felt. No matter a person's specific views on relationships or marriage, physical touch and intimacy are human needs, and studies have shown that being "skin hungry" can cause one to go crazy.[26] Everyone fills that void differently, and there's nothing wrong with a little D-squared as long as everyone's expectations are clear, but I recommend finding other ways to achieve touch without compromising your standards.

This phase passes, and a woman will realize she desires much more from a partner than merely a fun time. Even young women are thinking about more than a hookup when they're actually hooking up. According to a *Psychology Today* article about a study of "hook-up–experienced" undergrads, "65% of the women and 45% of the men said they hoped their hook-ups would *lead to long-term relationships*."[27] Hell, even Samantha Jones from *Sex and the City* slowed her pace and found a long-term relationship (for a while, at least). Eventually, there is a stronger desire for intimacy as opposed to sex, and there is a large difference. The sex may fade, but intimacy is what will keep you crawling across the table for your man many years down the road.

What do you desire the most, sex or intimacy, an HPA or a lasting relationship? Why can't you have both?
What are your standards around D-squared, HPA, and DR?

STAY SAFE, LADIES

Not to get too dark, here, but while we're talking about D-squared, HPA, and all that fun stuff, I'd be remiss if I didn't drop in a note about personal safety before we go too much further.

I had been dating for almost two years after the divorce when I was assaulted on a date. It took this event to learn how to set more boundaries, have more fierce conversations, and even gain more insight into myself. He was highly educated, held a respected position at work, and seemed kind, and our first couple of conversations had been fun and enlightening. We'd been talking for weeks, and we shared similar hobbies and common interests. For some reason, I let down my guard and let go of my rule to always meet first dates at a public place. Instead, I let him pick me up and drop me off at home.

I'm careful about when I let a man kiss me. I know that, in their minds, they often go straight from kissing you to sleeping with you. The key, I've found, is being sure you're confident before you make out with him that he respects you enough not to try to take it too far too soon. But even when you think you're safe, you may discover you're with a man who will try to go much farther. This was one of those men.

I had been assaulted once, in high school. That time, I froze. I could barely speak other than to say no, much less fight back. Like many others who've had a similar experience, I had played this scene in my head repeatedly for years, envisioning endless "what ifs." This time was different. This time I was not going to be a victim. This time I fought. I punched him repeatedly, so hard that he couldn't speak. When he got his wind back, he apologized repeatedly, asked that I never speak about what he did, and left. The #MeToo movement gave me the courage to fight back this time. It has provided the space for me to talk about my experiences without fear of judgment, and it has given me permission to let go of my shame. Finally, I found gratitude for the previous experience because it had enabled me to prevent more pain this time.

Many look at the #MeToo movement as a woman's issue, and there's a lot of power in that. But what if we looked at #MeToo as a men's issue too? Women are the ones who have said no, and men are the ones who have ignored it. What if this wasn't just about increasing the ways women have to protect ourselves but also about changing the way men behave? One of many upsides of the #MeToo movement is that, together, women are raising our standards for how we will be treated and what we will and will not accept, giving men no option but to change their perspectives, their choices, and their rhetoric.

It is difficult for a man to understand what it's like to fear dating. We always know where the entrances and exits are, and we never put our backs to the doors. We are ever vigilant of where a man's hands are, how we can escape every scenario, and who is within hearing distance of our calls for help. But what if we could relax just a little bit? What I know for sure is, gentlemen, #timesup!

There was a realtor in my market who was brutally kidnapped, raped, and murdered a few years ago. This inspired the Beverly Carter Foundation, which was formed in order to create safety standards in our industry to prevent future tragedies. As realtors who are often alone in homes with strangers, it makes sense that we should have serious safety standards. After the second assault, I started to implement these standards in my dating life too. These are the safety precautions I use while dating:

- Do not go meet someone from a dating platform without checking them out online first! Start by looking them up on Google, Facebook, and Instagram, but then go deeper. There is a wealth of public information available on just about anybody if you dig into county records, court records, online divorce decrees, criminal records, and property ownership records. There is no reason you shouldn't know more about these men than their mamas do. You should be one level below the FBI!

- If you are meeting someone for the first time, always meet at a public place, and let others know where you are going and who you are with. Have them text or call to check in on you, and text or call them when you leave or arrive home.
- Download an app like Circle of 6 to make it easy to let your friends know if you need help, or Scream Alarm to draw attention from bystanders if you get into trouble.
- If you're meeting someone at a bar, arrive early and make friends with the bartender. Form a signal that will notify the bartender to get you out of the date ASAP if things get uncomfortable or dangerous. (Many bars have systems like this set up—with codenamed drinks like "Angel Shot" that signal to bartenders you need help.)
- If you are at a bar or party, *always* take your drink with you everywhere you go! Do not leave your drink for your distracted girlfriends to watch—take it with you to the bathroom! Do not create any opportunities for someone to slip something into your drink.

And speaking of drinks and distracted girlfriends, here's a lighthearted little story about what might happen when you leave your belongings unattended in a bar. You know I've never been one to drink a lot of alcohol, so when I had two cocktails one night out with the girls, well, let's just say I was no longer fit to drive. I made the mistake of leaving my cell phone unlocked and in the hands of my closest girlfriends while I went to the restroom in my inebriated state. In my absence, these curious married friends of mine downloaded Tinder onto my phone and proceeded to choose my next husband, swiping only on men who were the complete opposite of me in every way! After an Uber ride home and what I thought was going to be a restful night's sleep, my phone started to blow up at five a.m. On a Saturday. That's when I discovered what my girlfriends had done. Most of my new "suitors" were waking up to go to shift work, and among them was a contender by the name of Rooster. The lesson? Never, ever leave your belongings—phone, drinks, anything—unattended! Yes, I was completely safe with my girlfriends, and this was a pretty innocuous prank, all things considered, but it was an eye-opening reminder of what can happen when you are in a compromised state and don't pay attention to your surroundings. So much for my wing women! But don't worry—I got my revenge by forwarding them the best of my Tinder messages in a group text, so they could all wake up to the "Rooster" also!

Men have to earn our trust over time, and we have to build our senses of safety and security with them at our own pace; neither should be freely given. Until then—and sadly, even after—we have to stay vigilant. And some self-defense classes never hurt.

SWIPE LEFT OR RIGHT?

Dating apps have a reputation of being all about D-squared and HPA. And they are fairly superficial, but when you learn to see through the bullshit of the pictures and blurbs, they do offer some indication of whether they're wet factor material. For example, there are some patterns in guys' photos that call for a quick left swipe or "Hell no" from me. Here is a brief and inexhaustive list:

Posing for every picture with the animals they have killed and caught. I do not want to vacation at deer camp, and I don't live for the next hunt. I have been hunting, and I have eaten wild game, but I have also evolved along with the rest of the species. I am not so primal that I find you attractive when you're covered in blood sitting next to a dead animal. Chances are, if he lives for the hunt, his other behaviors will be a little primal as well.

Choosing sports-related screen names. Have you ever noticed that at least 75% of dudes have screen names centered around sport teams? Now, I love a good Monday night football game—especially if Katie Sowers is coaching—but when their favorite sports are literally their identities, that's a no from me. Just ask their exes: I'm sure they will gladly tell you his evenings and weekends will be spent with ESPN instead of with you.

Drinking and partying in every picture. Someone needs to let these boys know their age and reiterate that we are not in college anymore. These guys tend to be sloppy with everything. *Next!* The constantly partying boys are similar to the never-fully-clothed boys. If you are looking for some D-squared, one of these might be your guy. But note, you are probably one of thirty he is chatting with.

Overcompensating with sunglasses, hats, filters, and other trick photography. The dude who is always wearing sunglasses is unattractive, and he knows it. The guy with a hat on in every picture is bald. If he's sitting down in every picture, or if they're all shot from the waist up, he is probably short. (If you ask how tall he is and he deflects, you know he's really short!) Pay attention to the background in the pictures. Being in the real estate field, I've learned to pay attention to surroundings more than others might. Any photos taken at home offer a bird's-eye view into how he keeps his house.

The modern version of hats, sunglasses, and seated shots are all these social media filters we can use to completely distort who we are! Talk about catfishing someone! I mean, I can go on

SnapChat, use what I call "the Botox filter," and look as young as my 11-year-old! When I'm 60, maybe I'll feel differently about the Botox filter, but until then, seeing someone using filters on their profile pics is a big red flag. Be authentic, people! Be aware that some men have been at this game a very long time and are extremely talented at taking pictures and writing descriptions that make them look much sexier, suaver, and swankier than they really are. This is why you must do your research. After you have wasted enough time on these boys, you will start to know what to look out for, and it will be much easier to eliminate the fakers.

If you think about it, these men are telling you a lot about themselves and their behaviors through their "best" pictures. I mean, if this is your best, then I really don't want to see your worst!

So what happens if you don't learn how to see past the social media curation and bullshit? You're likely to get catfished. I went on a date with a boy I met on Bumble. He was cute in his pictures, though nothing to get overly excited about. We had chatted for over a week, and we were going to have a drink. I arrived early. When he came in, he sat down and smiled really big, and I nearly fell off my barstool. He was missing a tooth! I had three options: 1) Drink, and drink a lot. 2) Get up and leave. 3) Ask questions and find the entertainment in the situation. I chose option 3.

Remember that episode of *Seinfeld* where Jerry goes on a date with a gorgeous woman, but all he can focus on are her man hands? She never acknowledges them and neither does he, but he's fixated. Well, ladies, this was my *Seinfeld* "Man Hands" moment! This dude continued to smile the entire date, and I couldn't focus on anything other than the gaping hole in his mouth! Was this going to be the hurdle I couldn't overcome? I had to know more. I had to ask questions! Surely there was an explanation, right?

I know poverty rates are high here in the Delta, but that was not his situation. Keep in mind, having sold real estate for more than seventeen years, I have an idea of property values all over town. So, when I ask a man where he lives, I automatically calculate the approximate appraisal value of his property. I very quickly found out that his parents lived in one of the few gated neighborhoods in town and that he had just sold a house that was worth anywhere between $600,000 and $1,000,000 based on its location. If he came from all this money, then why in the Sam Hell did he not have a tooth? Wouldn't you fix that before you went out with someone? Or wouldn't you at least use it as an ice-breaker? Why not address the elephant in the room, point out the fact that you're missing a tooth, and then explain what you're doing to get a new one? Nope, this dude continued to smile and chat like he didn't even know the tooth was gone. I thought maybe he'd gotten into a fight and had it knocked out recently, so I asked about his relationships and hobbies. All his responses were tame in nature—nothing violent. I never could flush out a plausible reason for the missing tooth, and he never said anything about it. After the date, I went back to look at his pictures on the app. Sure enough there were no pictures of that side of his face, and his mouth was closed in all his photos! This man presented himself as someone who was successful, came from a wealthy family, and had his own company…yet he was missing one of his front teeth and going on a first date in that condition as if he were first prize at the state fair. For me, that was a deal breaker.

Filters, trick photography, and catfishing aside, each of us wants what we want. It's the mix of attributes that makes somebody physically attractive. And yet, those attributes have to be there, in some combination, if we're going to move forward. So you have to answer this question, especially when you're dating in the age range of "middle age" or above: what are your physical expectations for a partner? You may be in the dad bod and receding hair market, you may no longer have a waist, and gray may be your new hair color, but you can still take care of yourself and look for partners who do the same. It cannot be overstated that beauty fades. But for me, teeth matter!

There will always be someone out there who is better looking, more successful, kinder, smarter, more thoughtful, more stable… the list goes on. The important question is, how does this person fulfill you? We have to have chemistry to develop real intimacy. If at any time during an intimate moment in the beginning of a relationship you think, "My vibrator can do better than this," then you need to cut him!

What physical characteristics are important to you?
What do your current or most recent partner's pictures tell
you about him, his habits, his lifestyle, and whether his
values align with yours?
What makes you swipe left right away?
What makes you swipe right?
How do you determine whether your partner has
the "wet factor?"

LOOKING FOR MORE THAN AN HPA

It is not lost on me that, when a man thinks about a woman, he is often thinking sexually. But when a woman thinks of a man, she thinks less about his penis and more about how he makes her feel. This is why, when the other pillars are not met, the wet factor will typically disappear fairly quickly for women. This is where many get tripped up by being so physically attracted to someone that they confuse that initial attraction for an indicator of sustainability. But when we learn to value others for more than what is on the surface, the wet factor becomes totally different. External beauty fades as we age, and the other values we share with our partners, such as intellectual depth, faith, empathy, or integrity, are what will build and sustain the wet factor. Don't get me wrong: I sure hope someone still slaps me on the ass when I'm in my 80s, but chances are it won't be because my skin is taught and my boobs are perky. The Huffington Post found those dating after 50 are more concerned with a potential partner's health and financial stability before they consider physical attraction.[28]

So take time to discover your true wet factor—what characteristics will get you going for the long term—and be sure he meets that standard *as well as* your other pillars. When you align in all these areas, the wet factor will be strong! The connection between two people has to be multilayered in order to make them knock the plates to the floor and crawl across the dinner table to ravage each other.

For me, at the end of the day, someone can look as if they came off a magazine cover and have a degree from Harvard, but if they can't make me laugh, I've got to cut 'em. Life has to be fun, and we have to keep the funny in everything we do. When a man can make me laugh, it turns up the wet factor to another level. We strive to surround ourselves with friends and coworkers we have a good time with, and choosing a mate is no different. No one ever included "Boring AF" on a wish list of traits they were seeking in a partner! Try putting that on a dating app, and see how many hits you get!

Chivalry and manners are important to me too. What the hell has happened to those? It's not enough just be pretty, gentlemen. If I wanted to look at something pretty, I would look in the mirror! I want a partner who is both pretty *and* chivalrous. And humble too. If they don't know how to get past their pretty, I cut 'em. The pretty ones are not accustomed to a woman who knows her value and what she wants in a partner. They are not accustomed to a woman who knows she has so much more than surface value to offer a man! But there is a lot of pretty out there, so don't let the pretty make you weak. The key is to find pretty with a brain and manners. That seems to be a feat.

Most of all, I don't do stupid! I cannot live the rest of my life with stupid! We are PowerWomen for a reason! A boy I have known since middle school continually messaged me on social media. I needed him to stop, so I told him I was dating someone. Unfortunately, that didn't work. Finally, when I had been nice for too long and he caught me at a bad moment, I said, "We are not a match, and you do not understand the trajectory I am on." His response told me everything! "What does trajectory mean?" Make sure his wit and intellect matches yours, or you will be bored within two months, tops! This is one great thing about online dating: you can read the profiles they write to check out their vocabulary and their grasp of what good writing looks like. It's not the only sign of smarts, but it's one indicator.

Now, there are two kinds of smart: classroom smarts and chutzpah. When a man can connect with, stimulate, and push a PowerWoman mentally, it is so hot! If his brain is on fire, we almost don't even need to see him to decide that he's hot. This is the explanation behind couples who are physically mismatched. You know exactly what I'm talking about. We have all been at the grocery and seen a stunningly beautiful woman with a not-so-hot man. We all know that beautiful friend whose spouse, though amazing in many ways, is not runway ready by any stretch. When people connect with one another through their intellects, that intimacy does not fade. The mind is so hot! If you are ever fortunate enough to find beauty *and* brains in a man, I say put a ring on it immediately!

How many marriages are built on lust alone? How many of those marriages end in divorce? The "wet factor" is a combination of both beauty and deeper-seated values. One does not come before the other, and which one you notice first likely depends on how you encounter your partner. How were you introduced? If you have known each other since childhood, you probably overlook a lot of physical aspects and are more likely to focus on the conversation, the intellect, and the deeper connection. If you meet on a dating app or online, you can certainly get a beat on what's beneath the surface, but chances are you match for physical reasons first.

The uniqueness of the wet factor was never more apparent to me than when I dated an incredibly brilliant man with a fascinating background and an Ivy League education. He was the epitome of classroom smarts. He was also very tall and overweight, and he walked like a duck. I didn't care. I craved our conversations, as he made me think, give me a different perspective, and made me laugh. He was real, and I allowed my masks to come off. He pursued me for months, and as I got to know him and learn about him, the wet factor became strong. Desire based on friendship and intellect is sustainable, and it is also hard to come by. I found it cute that he walked like a duck, and I never really saw his love handles. Unfortunately, he fell short in other pillars, but getting to know him highlighted for me that there is so much to be said for the depth of a wet factor that goes beyond a person's physical beauty.

If you have chutzpah, you have street smarts, grit, and hustle, and we PowerWomen respect that too. We want both! When a man has the combination of both classroom smarts and chutzpah, it takes the wet factor to the next level! If a man has the intelligence and the grit to keep up with me, I can respect him. And, ladies, if we can respect a man, then he will always register high on our wet factor! We want to be challenged by a man's brain, conversation, journey, mindset, growth, and grit!

Does this mean every man must be a Harvard graduate? No! Does this mean every man must be a workaholic? No! Many PowerWomen are married to stay-at-home dads, and this balance works beautifully for their families. These stay-at-home dads are brilliant too, and we all know parenthood requires chutzpah. We are who we surround ourselves with, and a man must bring his own brilliance to the table in order to challenge us. Whatever his career, if he is able to rise to the occasion and meet our growth, intellect, emotional capacity, and drive, then he will melt our butter all day long!

What do you find attractive in another?
What caused the wet factor to fade in your
failed relationships?
What do you desire the most from a partner?
What sustains your wet factor over time?
What do you desire from a relationship when you're 80?

GETTING COMFORTABLE IN YOUR OWN SKIN

When I had been in the Singlehood for over three years, one of my closest girlfriends took me to my first sex shop. I had no idea there were so many options for sex! My girlfriend was on a first-name basis with the people who worked there, but I was like a deer in headlights. For starters, I was absolutely shocked at the price tag on almost every item in the store. There was a huge glass counter similar to one you'd see at a jewelry store, and the items in there were the ones that most interested my friend. She and the employees started discussing performance, service options, and warranty information. Seriously? Did you know you could get your sex toys serviced or that they had warranties? As if my mouth wasn't on the floor already, in walked a lady requesting to pick up the items she had on hold. Excuse me? People called ahead and placed items on hold at the sex shop? I felt like I was caught between Nordstrom and the Dollar Store. This woman had ordered a gallon of lubricant. I didn't want to know why or how long it would last. Was there also layaway? As we left, I realized had never felt more grateful for Amazon! After becoming more comfortable with all of myself, the sex shop is now like Target for me—it is merely one more errand on my list.

Remember, I grew up very sheltered—and I remained very sheltered until after my divorce. I felt so awkward in that sex shop because I hadn't yet learned to be open about sex or be comfortable in my own skin. And, since then, I've discovered I wasn't alone. What I have learned about myself and many other women (whether they marry young like I did or not) is that we do not take time to discover our bodies. We were raised with a generation of women who did not discuss sex or introduce us to vibrators. But how can we have healthy sexual relationships if we do not get to know ourselves physically? And how can we empower ourselves to do just that? With a women's empowerment movement comes sexual empowerment, meaning it's time to stop slut shaming each other and embrace our sexuality in all forms. Giving yourself permission to love and enjoy all of life is freeing, and if that means frequenting the sex shop each month then I say *hell yes*!

Women often do not know what we have to offer in the sexual arena because we are not comfortable in our own skin. Sometimes that comfort comes with age, a particular event, or the self-reflection that finally empowers us to love our bodies and know that allowing others to experience them is like awarding a serious prize. Once we've developed this comfort, listening to younger women discuss their bodies is heart-wrenching. When I remember what I thought about my own body as a young teenager, I think, *"Damn, you looked good! What were you thinking?!"* I didn't put on a bikini between the ages of 16 and 34. But it was so liberating to finally look in the mirror and fall in love, despite the age spots, with the mother and woman I have become! Wouldn't it be wonderful if we gifted our daughters with steadfast bodily self-confidence and self-love that did away with body dysmorphia throughout their lives? This realization came to me in full force when I had a shopping experience at a local boutique in town.

It was early on a weekday morning, the boutique had just opened, and I needed a dress for an upcoming event. There were two beautiful, thin young girls who looked to be in college opening the store. When they opened their mouths, I had flashbacks to the movie *Clueless*. They were transplants from Beverly Hills,

I swear! I went into the dressing room to try on my items while they chatted about their newest diet. It went like this:

Girl 1: OMG! Have you tried the new orange diet? You don't eat anything orange!

Girl 2: No! So no Cheetos?

Girl 1: Yeah, like, you don't eat carrots or sweet potatoes or anything orange! 'Cause of all the sugar. You know when you cook carrots and they're sweet, it's because they're full of sugar, so they'll make you fat! So no orange is no sugar!

Girl 2: Oh, right! All the sugar!

Girl 1: Yeah, so, sugar turns to fat, so you don't eat sugar so you don't get fat!

The conversation continued, but I had had enough of it! I came out of the dressing room and intervened.

Girl 1: How did everything work for you?

Me: Sorry, nothing fit right today. But I want to chat with you about the new orange diet!

Girl 1: Oh yeah, totally!

Me: Yeah! You girls are stunningly beautiful in ways you aren't even seeing! Appreciate it. Eat orange foods! Eat whatever foods you want! And *please* eat all the carrots you can get your hands on! Your eyes will thank you later. Last, take lots of pictures of yourselves now, because one day you'll look back and appreciate yourself!

After I left, it hit me: why in the world was I not taking my own advice? Why do women struggle to value all of ourselves throughout our entire journeys? Why are we always nitpicking and finding fault with ourselves? I took my own advice and called a photographer I trusted while I was in the parking lot. I booked a photo session for that week. Many women have boudoir photos taken as gifts for their significant others. But I wasn't dating anyone, and I had these made for me. I had discovered myself, my body, and all of who I was becoming as a woman, and I wanted to capture that.

Sex is powerful, and we deserve it! When we learn to love and appreciate all of ourselves, we can allow others to appreciate us sexually as an act of love.

Are you loving and appreciating all of yourself in order to allow someone else to do the same?
What do you desire a sexual relationship to look like?
What do you love about your body?
What parts of yourself are you working to embrace?

LESSONS OF A SINGLE MOM

As always, we are the models for our children, and conversations around sex and dating can be tricky. Everyone's choices are different and should be respected. Do you live together before marriage? Do you sleep over while dating? What standard are you setting, and does it align with the message you are telling your children? If you are preaching abstinence while your boyfriend is staying the night, what does that say to your children? Many of us do not consider the sexual choices we're modeling until we find ourselves having these conversations with our preteens or teenagers. Do your actions align with your message? Being a dating parent creates a wonderful opportunity to model a healthy dating relationship dynamic you hope your children will emulate. No pressure! Are they seeing you put on a fancy dress to go to dinner, or are they seeing your boyfriend come over late at night and leave early in the morning? How are you using your experiences with sex in the dating space as a conversation to empower your children?

SEVEN

Are You Faux Real?

One day I was at the shampoo stand at the salon, listening to another girl talking to her stylist about her husband. She was reminiscing about their pre-marriage dating life, and the following statement came out of her mouth: "You know, after I got him hooked, then I could be myself all the time." I was floored! I couldn't believe she'd just said that out loud! I interjected, because she and the rest of the salon had to know that pretending to be something you're not is no way to "hook" a man of character.

Approaching dating like it's a game will never work if you want to meet someone of character, grit, and worth. The law of attraction is real on many levels, and dating is no different. When someone sees you—your real, authentic self—and connects with you, accepts you, desires you, and pursues you, *that* is a magical relationship. This, ladies, is worth gold! And yet the behavior this other woman was talking about, trying to be somebody else to attract a partner, is all too common among both men and women. We see it all over the place, in movies, on TV, in books, and on the news.

As women today, it can feel like we wear many masks. We're prim and proper at a black-tie fundraiser, loud and boisterous at a football or little league game, and direct and professional in the corporate world. Sometimes it feels like the only person we rarely get to be is our authentic self. Taking off the masks—yes, *all* of them—to be our authentic selves and allowing someone else to be a true partner in all things requires a high level of vulnerability!

One of the reasons this is so difficult is that, as women, we often struggle so much with imposter syndrome that we hide our authentic selves for fear that, at any moment, somebody will realize we're not "good enough" after all. And this struggle creeps into our dating life, which keeps many of us single or dating the wrong boys for decades! In dating, imposter syndrome keeps us second guessing whether or not we deserve someone who meets our standards (much less exceeds our expectations), and this keeps us from being vulnerable and authentic. But the reality is, we must let go of what holds us back and realize that we are worthy of more than we can imagine. This allows us to love ourselves enough to be authentic and vulnerable without shame. If we don't allow ourselves to be ourselves, then we'll find our relationships don't last. So many times, when people get caught up in the hype of being attached, they try to become somebody that they are not in order to squeeze into what looks like an ideal relationship. But after a while, their true authentic self comes out, and *boom*! They're right back on Tinder! But when a woman risks trusting and being her true, authentic self with a man and he still chases her, then he becomes a real contender! When the foundation of a relationship is authentic friendship, that's something magical. But it is not something you will find by merely reading profiles on a dating app. It takes a lot more effort than that to discover your person.

Have I opened myself up to men, taken off my masks, been my authentic self, and allowed those men to love me for me? Yes.

How did that work for me? It hasn't been easy, but it's been awesome, because it's led to powerful learning, growth, friendship, and enlightenment during my journey in the Singlehood. And it's also helped me weed out boys who aren't willing or able to embrace me for all that I really, truly am.

Of course, you may wonder how I can call those authentic moments successful if I'm not married or in a "permanent" partnership. Well, that's just because none of the men who've loved me for my authentic self have also met my other pillars, and that's important! When we feel comfortable enough with a man to be our true authentic selves, we *can* fall into the trap of ignoring the pillars. We are looking for someone to love and accept us for who we truly are, and when someone sees our authenticity and sticks around we get weak in the knees. But, while that's a critical component of a healthy relationship, it's only one component.

LESSONS OF A SINGLE MOM

For single moms, it can be especially difficult to allow ourselves to be vulnerable with others and disclose our authentic selves. Being a single mom in the first place most likely means that a close relationship has dissolved for one reason or another. In other words, we've typically built taller and stronger walls around ourselves and our children, and we require an extreme amount of trust to be vulnerable with someone else! Full authenticity means showing a potential partner how we parent and, eventually, introducing him to our children. This does not happen quickly or easily, because PowerMoms are highly protective of our children. It takes us a great deal of time to build trust and let our walls down, and that's ok. Take your time, and don't let anybody pressure you to move faster, because showing our vulnerability as single parents is a difficult, emotional step that should not be taken lightly.

BEING YOUR TRUE SELF, DESPITE OTHERS' EXPECTATIONS

If we aren't willing to be our true, authentic selves, then by default, we hand over the power to society and the partners we choose to set expectations for who we should become. Rather than focusing on becoming our most powerful, confident selves, we'll be stuck trying to live up to the images others have created for us. How miserable is that? And besides, frankly, the expectations that go with being a woman are overwhelming at times. If we leave our identities up to others, those expectations will control and paralyze us. What would it look like if we let go of other peoples' expectations and set our own, instead? Until women choose to take control of the expectations we and others have for ourselves, we will be stuck making the same old choices, and society will never change to our benefit! It's time to embrace our authenticity in order to drive change and move the pendulum.

Mother Wikipedia states that we achieve authenticity when our actions are congruent with our desires.[29] Many women fear being their authentic selves because they fear judgment. (Judgment from men, yes, but let's be clear: women are also the worst about tearing each other apart. What gives, ladies?) We are expected to look fabulous at any given moment and never stretch beyond a size two (no matter how recently we delivered that baby). Many women feel the need to apply a face, a gown, and heels just to go to the grocery store, and some women feel like they're putting on a dog and pony show every time they leave the house. And don't even get me started on how cute we're supposed to look while we work out. We still hear too many half-serious jokes about how women should be seen and not heard and how a woman's place is in the kitchen. We're supposed to have thriving careers (that don't intimidate our husbands or male colleagues), perfect children, flourishing social and romantic relationships, Pinterest-worthy houses, and the perfect outfit for every occasion. Trying to be and do everything we're supposed to be and do is exhausting, and it's no wonder many women constantly feel like they're just trying to avoid being judged for that one little slipup. Yet all any of us desire is to be accepted at the end of the day. Ladies, what would it look like if we shook off those expectations and chose who and what we want to be without judgment? What if society not only accepted us but supported our choices to live authentically?

Big picture, there are two main things our society fails to embrace for women: power and aging. We're always balancing precariously on that razor-thin line between striving for success and not looking so successful that we become intimidating or undesirable. And we're constantly spending wild amounts of money and bending over backward to look ten years younger or ten pounds thinner. Take Spanx, for example. If you have never tried on a pair of Spanx, I challenge you to put one on and wear it for three hours while you go about your day. Now, don't get me wrong: I'm all about wearing the proper undergarments to avoid lines under your clothes, but for the most part, I believe women have taken Spanx and other Spanx-like products too far.

Too many of us wear them to look two sizes smaller, fitting into both that little black dress and society's expectations. As a result, we run around feeling constricted and grumpy and hot (not in the good way but the soaked-in-sweat way) all day long. Is peeing from a slit in your britches really authentic?

Remember the warning I gave earlier about pretending you're something you're not in order to get into a relationship? Eventually, your authentic self comes out and you and your partner realize it's not a match after all. Spanx are the physical embodiment of that falsehood: you pretend to be or look or feel a certain way, but when the Spanx come off and you're finally free to breathe and be yourself, your partner realizes you're not what he thought. This isn't to say that who you really are is unworthy. It's *so worthy!* But when you make a match and build a relationship based on false identity—when you squeeze your heart and soul into metaphorical Spanx—it's bound to fall apart eventually. So let's imagine, for a moment, a world without Spanx. What would it look like if we celebrated a woman for speaking her truth, being a voice for others, loving herself, and building the life she truly desires? What if those were the qualities we held up as attractive?

We give men a lot of flak for perpetuating these harsh, unreachable expectations, and they deserve it for sure. But in reality, the harshest critics of women are almost always other women! We fall prey over and over to something called Queen Bee Syndrome, in which we treat each other terribly because we feel like there's only room for one woman at the top, and the only way we can succeed is to shove all our fellow ladies back down.[30] We judge each other, especially those who have excelled or are in leadership positions, and we rip each other to the bone! Heaven forbid a woman breastfeed in public! Heaven forbid a woman not breastfeed at all! Get over it already! Feed the babies—feed all the babies! Who cares how or when or where?

Women also shame other women for working, for being stay-at-home mothers, for dating, for not dating, for dating the "wrong way," and anything else we can think of, it seems. When are we going to start listening to ourselves? We fight for freedom of choice over our bodies. Then we shame each other for making choices we disagree with. And in the end? We just perpetuate every stereotype and every unrealistic expectation, and nobody wins. But when we choose to let go of judgment and approach all people with curiosity and respect, then we can finally give each other and ourselves permission to live our own authentic truths. It may not be perfect, but the reality is that, as women, we have a lot of freedom today. If we would only let go of others' expectations, our fear of judgment, and our awful tendency to tear each other down, there's no limit to what we could achieve. We now have the choice to be the CEO in the boardroom or the stay-at-home mother who home schools her children. Either choice, or any choice in between, is fantastic as long as we're making those choices based on our own authentic truths. We are all Queen Bees, and if we can all learn to step into our uniqueness and live authentically, there will be room for all of us at the top. What if we were all more like Idgie Threadgoode from the movie *Fried Green Tomatoes*—Bee Charmers rather than Queen Killers?

Sometimes it comes with age, and sometimes is comes with self-discovery, but eventually we will all get to the point where we no longer care about judgment and are able to walk through the fear. We do this by learning to love and accept our true selves and recognizing our opportunities for growth. Letting go of fear is the most liberating feeling. It allows us to achieve goals others never thought we could achieve. This is the gift we need to share with others and use to empower our daughters. We can have fear, or we can have faith, but we cannot have both!

If you choose to not live authentically,
what will you fail to achieve?
Who will you fail to help?
Have you been hiding any qualities you're
now ready to embrace?

Some qualities are admirable, some are beautiful, and some are sexy, but the most irresistible quality a woman can flaunt is her authenticity! There is nothing more attractive or sexy to a man of quality than a woman who is confident in herself and her own skin! A series of 2019 studies discussed in *Psychology Today* have shown that, when we are authentic with one another, then we can feel safe and begin to lay the groundwork for a long-lasting relationship.[31] But when we sense others are not being authentic, we play hard-to-get and hold back our own authentic selves, turning dating into a game. It begs the question, are you really mating or only dating?

So what are the signs of inauthenticity in a potential partner? Interestingly enough, the same studies cite someone's willingness to introduce you to their friends or family as a key indicator of authenticity. Getting to know other people in a man's life provides insight into how he is when you're not around. There is an amazing bachelor I know who dated a woman more than twenty years younger for years. All of us have seen this scenario: hot, successful man dating the young, beautiful woman. Many of us roll our eyes and move on, but what if we took a closer look? During a business meeting with this man, I learned that, after two years of dating this woman and traveling the world on romantic getaways, he had never introduced her to his children or told his parents how old she was. In other words, as far as anyone else in this man's life was concerned, she was just a place card. Despite how much he enjoyed her company, his refusal to show her his authentic self—including his choice to hide her from his family—prohibited them from forming a long-lasting relationship. How do you want to show up in a relationship, and are you willing to let go of the fear, equip yourself with courage, and step into authenticity in order to have a mate, or do you want to maintain strict boundaries and simply date? You choose! What I know for sure is that I will never be anyone's place card!

Allowing someone to see and know your authentic self opens the door to a deeper stage of love and commitment. Every discussion I've read about the phases of love includes a phase of authenticity or trust building, and this stage is identified as the key to a sustainable relationship.

LESSONS OF A SINGLE MOM

When are we going to give ourselves permission not to do the laundry? As mothers, we place unrealistic expectations on ourselves to create a "Holiday Card life," and then when we fall short, we feel a sense of failure. For example, moms are supposed to be in "boob jail," according to the La Leche organization, and breastfeed for at least a year after delivery while we juggle the kids we already have, sport schedules, meal planning, laundry, housekeeping, work schedules and deadlines, our spouses, "me" time, fitness, a social life, community involvement, and, hopefully, a little time to pray for sanity.[32]

But studies have shown that this unrealistic pressure is causing burnout, and women are not fulfilling their career ambitions.[33] So let go of the insane expectations and consider what is right for you. Are you winning as long as you get the kids to school on time, even if they eat breakfast in the car and you are in your robe? Are you winning even if you haven't showered in days, but you wear your pearls to the grocery store? What if a dirty house meant you were focused on time with your children? What if career success meant you were able to provide educational opportunities for your children? How do you need to reframe your expectations in order to achieve your potential?

We live in fear of not meeting expectations at work because we are mothers. How do you balance breastfeeding and the boardroom? How do you prepare for a large work project when you're helping with homework, cooking dinner, and tucking children into bed? Getting rid of the mommy guilt feels impossible, but what I know for sure is that we place that guilt on ourselves. What if a stranger said the things to you that you say to yourself? Do you speak to yourself with the same love and grace you give your children?

Now, imagine maintaining the standards society has set for women without a partner. The expectations placed on single parents is immense. Many single parents feel a paralyzing sense of guilt at not meeting those expectations, and they overcompensate with their children in different—and usually unhealthy—ways. It is ok not to be able to do it all and have it all at the same time. I will never be the "Hallmark Mother" at my children's school. I attend many school parties, and I volunteer as much as possible, but I can't do it all. I also negotiate millions of dollars in contracts on a weekly basis. I am a force! I do not have the time or energy to make Valentine's Day goodie bags! And if you don't either, that's ok! My kids go to aftercare, and if yours do too, that's ok! This does not mean my love for motherhood is any less. I cherish my children, moment by moment. I have frequent conversations with my children to ensure they will always know how much they are loved and that everything I do is with the intent to help better their lives.

I value their words, their growth, and who they are becoming as people, and I worry about how I can equip them to become better. My daughter says to me almost daily, "Mommy, you're the best." I always respond to her, "And, my dear, you will be better!"

DEFINING THE WOMAN YOU WANT TO BE

It took that trip to the club with the girls to realize I had quit living life to the fullest. I had quit being my authentic self. Did I really enjoy cooking, or did I do it because my ex had always asked what was for dinner? Did I want to live in the area of town we lived in, or had I defaulted to that based on someone else's expectations? No, I was not that deep in thought at the club, but when I got home I realized there was so much I had not experienced. There was so much of life I had chosen not to participate in because I was comfortable in mediocrity. Was that the legacy I wanted to leave for my children? *Hell no!*

As I started to see my blind spots in life, I made a "living life list" of experiences I wanted to embrace. This was not an elaborate list, and to this day it remains a living document, as it is ever changing as I check off and add events. As I started checking off small, simple things I had never tried or accomplished, I discovered that life was fun and full of adventure again! I had found my inner child and my path to authenticity! If you feel like you're stuck in a rut or you're struggling to find your authentic self, I encourage you to make a "living life list," and then get to work! Here are a few items from the beginning of my three-page list:

- Have a man ask for my phone number
- Have a man take me to dinner
- Travel by myself
- Travel with the children by myself
- Go skinny dipping
- Go camping
- Travel abroad
- Do something spontaneous I would have never done in the last ten years
- Start a journal
- Go to lunch/dinner/cocktails with someone new every month to learn their story

It is amazing what happens to us when we start taking chances and letting our inner authenticity come out. We start to notice the little things in life. I started to hear the birds in the morning, even before daylight. I hadn't heard the birds in years, and now their early morning song is the most beautiful music I have ever heard. I was hearing and seeing the world in a new beautiful way.

It is like when you get glasses for the first time, and you can finally see the leaves on the trees. The cloud had been lifted from my life, and the birds were singing! This was what liberation felt like! I was no longer anyone else's story. I was me.

But finding that inner authenticity isn't easy, especially as we juggle everyone else's ideas about who we are. Isn't it interesting to see how others view us? Always in relation to someone else in our lives, often without even a first or last name. You're someone's boss or coworker or realtor or date or girlfriend. There's a whole group of people—both children and adults—who only know me as "Caroline's Mom." All these identities may be true, and we may take pride in all of them, but they don't encompass our authentic selves. When we embrace our authenticity, when we find our joy, then others will connect us with that. But first, we have to find it ourselves.

How do you want people to finish the sentence,
"Oh, you're the woman who…?"
What do you want to be known for?
What represents who you really are?

Somewhere along the way, women have accepted that it is ok to settle in all areas of our lives. When we're little girls, we're told we can do anything we want. But as we get older, the field of opportunity starts to shrink. Then suddenly, that inner voice of empowerment disappears. Why? Who told you that you should settle? Whose negativity was so impactful in your life? When did your mindset change? When did you start to view yourself differently? Who told you "no," and why did you listen?

When women settle, we lose track of our authenticity. We

lose our sense of adventure, wonderment, and curiosity, and we get into a rut. So many times, the overwhelming aspects of everyday life take hold and, before you know it, you've lost the core of who you are. Snap out of it! Get out of your sweats, and find who you are supposed to become!

One of the battles we face as we determine who we want to be is a battle between our sense of self and the expectations versus realities of our own femininity. It seems impossible to remain feminine when masculinity tends to rise into leadership and accomplish change, yet when we do try on more masculine traits, we're criticized for being too aggressive or too serious or too unfriendly. So, are we to embrace masculinity or femininity? Are we supposed to be short and curvy to make our men feel masculine, or tall and lithe to match the models we see in magazines? Are we supposed to be Suzy Homemakers or modern feminists? Are we supposed to stay likeable or lean in? How can we command respect like men do without being too formidable? How are we to be powerful in today's world and maintain our feminine identity as women?

As women, our real power and attraction lie in our authentic femininity—whatever that may look like for you. This is what, ultimately, is most attractive to a worthy man, but it's also the feature we tend to hold back the most or struggle to define for ourselves. When we embrace the vulnerability that comes with accepting and leveraging our authentic femininity, then we will have freedom of choice in the dating space and everywhere we choose to succeed.

Let me stop a second and explain what I mean when I refer to authentic femininity. I'm not suggesting that we all have to be 1950s housewives (though if that's what really melts your butter, then go for it, darlin'). Rather, I'm contradicting this idea that, in order to be powerful and successful, we have to act like men. That we have to shout and posture and play "I am woman hear me roar." How often have we seen these tactics backfire for women? Instead, I encourage all of us to embrace our authentic personalities—and especially the feminine characteristics that give us so much power when we learn how to leverage them. When we choose to rest in our softness and femininity, that's when we can really move the pendulum! For example, we often feel like we have to put on our "man voices" if we want to be heard—talking over others and filling every gap in conversation with our opinions and commentary like a man might. But if we combat that urge and rest instead in that feminine ability to use quiet to make a point, then we're that much closer to getting our way.

Legally Blonde's Elle Woods is one of the most extreme—and most fantastic—examples of a woman fully embracing her femininity to achieve her goals, no matter how many people tell her to tone it down. Sure, she had a lot of learning and growing to do, but she knew better than to compromise her true self. She maintained her feminine empathy, loyalty, and style no matter what. The image of her walking down the courthouse steps, signature pink dress and bouncy blond curls, telling reporters that she knew Chutney was guilty because "the rules of haircare are simple and finite. Any Cosmo girl would have known" is such a powerful illustration of how far our femininity can get us in life. Of course, we don't all need to mimic Elle Woods in order to use our femininity to our advantage. Let's look at a few other women—real and fictional—who've leveraged their femininity to outshine every man in the room, achieving their goals without compromising who they are.

Julia Robert's did this twice—once as Erin Brockovich in *Erin*

Brockovich and once as Katherine Watson in *Mona Lisa Smile*. In
Erin Brockovich, Erin's boss, Ed, tries to make her conform to the
stereotypes for her role as a paralegal, suggesting that she might
want to rethink her wardrobe a little. But Erin refuses to compromise: "Well as long as I have one ass instead of two, I'll wear
what I like if that's all right with you." Later on, still not having
compromised on her appearance, she uses the power of silence
to negotiate a rehire, raise, and benefits from Ed. While any of us
might be tempted to "man up" and argue our case, she embraces
her quiet femininity. And lo and behold, she gets exactly what
she asks for—and she takes down PG&E while she's at it. When
a confounded Ed asks what makes her so confident that she can
get what she wants all the time, she replies softly, "They're called
boobs, Ed." Know the power of your femininity, rest in it, and
leverage it to its highest potential!

In the movie *Mona Lisa Smile*, Julia Roberts does it again,
this time as Katherine Watson, an art teacher helping women
push their own definitions of femininity beyond the classroom
at Wellesley College. The movie is set in 1953, when women
were starting to expand their potential outside of the kitchen and
unlock other opportunities through education. Watson empowers her students to embrace their freedom of choice, remaining
"ladylike" but finding and using their own voices and skills to
build the lives they want. Interestingly enough, the standards of
femininity for the women in this film mirror the way we define
them today: gentleness, empathy, humility, and sensitivity.

Today, Katie Sowers is making history as the first female coach
in the Superbowl and the first openly gay NFL coach in history.
And how did she get there? Not by trying to act like a man, but
by being her whole self and understanding the power she has as

a woman. In her Microsoft Surface Pro commercial, Sowers says, "People tell me that people aren't ready to have a woman lead, but these guys have been learning from women their whole lives: moms, grandmas, teachers…"[34]

And, finally, perhaps the most amazing woman I've ever encountered: Justice Ruth Bader Ginsburg. This incredible woman raised a 2-year-old while attending Harvard Law School, where she was one of just nine women among three hundred students, all while she helped her husband battle cancer and graduate with his own Harvard Law degree. I had the opportunity to hear Justice Ruth Bader Ginsberg be interviewed recently, and as I listened to her educate the audience about the gender equality cases she has argued in front of the United States Supreme Court and how she has helped move the pendulum for women, I couldn't help but notice that she seemed very grounded and comfortable in her own personality, and that she has never sacrificed her natural femininity in order to make a difference; instead, she's used it to make herself more powerful. Ginsburg is one of the most influential women in our country, and yet she doesn't present herself as loud and boisterous in the way many male leaders do. When I saw her, she was mild-mannered, quick-thinking, and deliberate in her speech. (Not to mention she was wearing heels and black lace gloves at 86-years-old!)

Her story and presence were powerful, but not because she assumed any masculine characteristics. As she discussed her vulnerability in her life's most difficult moments, she displayed strength, compassion, and sensitivity. Ginsburg has leveraged her authentic femininity to move mountains in a masculine world, changing the laws of gender equality in our country. This is not to say that Ruth Bader Ginsburg's style of femininity is the only effective style. She may not have been as successful if she had approached feminism by marching in a midriff and leather pants, but that's because that approach doesn't jibe with her authentic self. If marching is your authentic style, then march, darlin'! But know that, if your natural approach is softer, quieter, and more traditionally feminine, you, too, have the power to leverage your authentic traits to elicit change.

In today's society, we often find ourselves torn between putting up the hard exterior persona of "PowerWoman" in order to climb the corporate ladder or painting a highly feminine, Norman Rockwell-style picture of our lives in order to attract men. But remember what's most attractive: our authentic femininity—whatever that means to each of us. If you're more comfortable in a pantsuit and pearls, rock them. If you prefer dresses and lace, embrace them. Either way, when we learn how to leverage our authentic traits and our unique approaches to femininity—casting aside anyone else's expectations or our own mistaken instinct that we have to "act like a man" to get where we want to go—we will have the power to both succeed in any area we choose *and* attract a man of quality who meets our standards and loves us for who we truly are.

What does femininity look like to you?
How are you choosing to rise within your femininity?
What is your unique femininity, and
how are you leveraging it?

BEING VULNERABLE IS A STRENGTH

Being vulnerable is one of the many feminine traits that's gotten a bad rap in the business world—and in other areas of life, too. But

I'm here to tell you that vulnerability is a strength. We observe promising leaders who rise in their careers only to plateau—or even fall—because they wear a heavy armor of self-protection.

The queen of relationships, Brené Brown, whom I fondly refer to as "Mother Brené," is transforming our thinking regarding vulnerability. She challenges her audiences to analyze our fear of being vulnerable with others. I've watched Mother Brené's TED Talk about the power of vulnerability on repeat over the years, and she has ingrained in me the belief that our resistance to being vulnerable in our relationships comes from the shame we carry and our fear of not being accepted and losing the connections we desire with others.[35] In other words, we hold back in our relationships rather than opening up about our dark and dirty because we're afraid that, if we do, the other person won't stick around. But what would it look like if we anticipated the opposite? What if we let go of our fears and became transparent in our relationships, confident that doing so will help us become even more connected? What I had to learn was that, when I accepted my own shame and loved myself fully, then I was able to be vulnerable with another in order to create intimacy and space for love. I no longer feared losing a relationship or a connection because my relationship with myself filled my whole heart, and a relationship with another became a bonus. This is the power of vulnerability!

What is the armor you use to protect yourself?
How are you choosing to hide from
being vulnerable with others?
How are you choosing to step into the arena?

I had been seeing a man for only two months when I had to

go to the hospital with kidney stones, and this man showed up. I wasn't able to drive, walk, or eat, and I sure didn't look my best. Darlin', I was diving head first into the vulnerability deep end! After hours in the ER and multiple doses of pain medication, I finally birthed the stone. There were no secrets, and he'd even learned my full medical history. His response? This man brought me takeout from Waffle House and watched *Sex and the City* with me the rest of the day. Through his presence during one of my most vulnerable moments, this man revealed his own authenticity, and it was magic. There was nothing I couldn't do, say, or be around him. I could be all of me, without fear, and this created a different level of intimacy. I discovered a different connection because I allowed myself to be vulnerable with him. Unfortunately, we later learned that we didn't fight well, which is an important element in every successful relationship, so we ran our course. But this experience taught me valuable lessons that I've carried into every relationship since. Mostly, that Mother Brené is always right.

Imagine the most vulnerable situation you could be in, and then imagine the man you are dating is there next to you. When you choose to let him in, you'll see his authenticity and experience the power that vulnerability has to show you the strength of your relationship. Then, when a man allows you to see him in his most vulnerable state, you have the opportunity to love him—and all his imperfections—fully.

What type of connection do you desire?
How vulnerable you choose to be determines the depth of
your connection. Are you ready to let someone in?

Traditionally, the higher a PowerWoman rises in her career, the more alone she becomes. No one prepares us for this. Additionally, when we raise our standards, we find the selections grow slim. We will not date our clients, coworkers, or any men who do not meet our pillars. But the relative isolation of career success, combined with the slim pickings for partners, has the potential to drop us right back into the Lonely. Fortunately, this is also an opportunity for tremendous growth. Our sense of self-preservation has allowed us to achieve such greatness in business, but it will sabotage personal relationships. In our efforts to further our careers, our self-preservation instincts have made us extremely guarded creatures, and this can carry over into our personal lives. Unfortunately, being "tough as nails and hard to crack" will get us nowhere in the dating world, and we will probably cut some promising prospects too soon because we are too guarded. While certain walls have served us well in the boardroom, we must also learn to soften ourselves, let down our walls, and welcome vulnerability in personal relationships.

Life is too short not to live and love. If we do not allow ourselves to enjoy what the world has to offer, we will miss amazing opportunities! Which is greater, the interminable pain of the Lonely or the temporary pain of heartbreak? When you choose to put on the armor each day, you're resigning yourself to living in the Lonely. But when you opt to be vulnerable, you set yourself up for powerful connections—romantic and otherwise—and a life filled with joy. The worst you'll experience is the temporary pain of heartbreak. But, ladies, we've all been through it before, and we know we can always bounce back.

When we embrace the power of vulnerability and authenticity in the dating space, we give ourselves permission to throw away the armor and step into the dating arena with the intent of building connections and nurturing love. It's not easy, but by allowing others to see the pain and damage life has thrown at us, we're also showing them the incredible growth we have achieved. Allowing and committing to vulnerability is the only way to create real, deep, and true relationships. Do not fear the vulnerability, but share it, learn from it, and grow from it. Letting someone in doesn't diminish our status as PowerWomen—it strengthens us! When we hide our suffering and our faults, we prevent ourselves from growing, nurturing ourselves and others, and building authentic connections.

Have you had to put up walls to grow your career?
How have they affected your personal life?
What's one thing you can do to bring more vulnerability
into your relationships?

Letting go of fear unlocks the door to success in all aspects of life. In order to achieve deep connectivity, you must push through the fear, move forward in faith, and be your authentic self with others. Follow your passion, rediscover your authenticity, and be vulnerable with your connections, and you'll ultimately attract the right partner—someone who will align with your pillars and support you in your journey. You are capable of more than you can fathom, and the more you embrace your vulnerable, authentic self, the more others will see it!

Mommy Warbucks

Logic makes you think, and emotions make you act. Many times when we are in relationships, we let our emotions overcome our logic, causing our circle of friends to shake their heads and start placing bets on how long our second marriage will last. Looking for evidence of how complete logic tends to escape us when we're dating? Consumer Reports says that the FBI identifies romance fraud as more costly to consumers than any other type of Internet fraud.[36] Consumers lost over $230 million in Internet dating fraud in 2016 alone, and the FBI even anticipates that their numbers are low because many victims are too embarrassed to report. Even scarier? These crazy numbers don't even account for offline dating fraud.

So, as PowerWomen who work hard for our money, how are we to be vulnerable and still keep armor around our checkbooks? How much do you respect your money, and how much does *he* respect your money? Come to think of it, which is he more interested in: you or your money? When you're spending money in your relationships, are you spending emotionally or logically?

Mutual friends introduced me to a man who was deployed with the military. Before I knew it, I was receiving phone calls from a base abroad. Our phone calls, texts, and Face-time sessions went on for five months, and I was so in love with being in love that I allowed myself to be vulnerable. Looking back, I know there were red flags that should have given me pause: let's just say, multiple patterns of financial insecurity. And yet, I disregarded all of that, filtering out everything but the words I wanted to hear. (The fact that he was far away overseas made it even easier.) Gifts arrived in the mail periodically, and the constant attention from a man was new and exciting.

I was so infatuated, in fact, that when he had leave from his deployment, I met him in Europe. Most of the women in my circle cautioned me against going, but I was excited about a trip to Europe. And I wasn't disappointed either! Well, not with Europe at least. My vacation was filled with history, and everything was enchanting and beautiful. The man, however, was a different story. I immediately started to see the red flags I'd been ignoring, along with new signs that something wasn't right, and we fell into fierce conversations throughout the week that gave me pause. I learned his financial history was even less stable than he'd presented it, and he had greater financial insecurity than I'd realized. I was reminded that, when it comes to dating, there is no substitute for spending time in person with a potential partner, as that is when we can really get a good look at one another, inside and out.

I knew early in the trip that this relationship wasn't going anywhere, but he had one more surprise in store. As we were packing our bags on our last evening together, he asked me for money. A lot of money. My jaw dropped. I turned around in disbelief, speechless. Fortunately, he answered his own question for me: "Oh, I guess I shouldn't ask you that since you told me you wouldn't marry me till I got my shit together." I'm not one to hold my tongue, but there have been a few moments in my life when I've known that, if I spoke, I would do too much damage. This was one of them. I was in shock, and I knew silence was best for both of us. I continued packing, never said a word, and never gave him a dime.

While his ask was undoubtedly unacceptable and unprovoked, the truth was that, somehow, I had let this man feel comfortable enough with me to ask for the money. Of course, the real blame was on his own lack of self-respect and inability to "get his shit together," but as I reflected, I realized that I could learn some things from this crazy scene about setting my own standards. I had compromised for this man. I had not firmly established my standards for respect, and, consequently, he didn't feel as if he had done anything wrong. I had ignored red flags and made excuses, acting emotionally because I was in love with being in love. I had been ignoring his manipulation rather than demanding respect for months, but it was time to act with logic, not emotion. I was not going to be a Consumer Report statistic! When we arrived at the airport after eight hours of almost-complete silence, I was finally able to formulate a logical question: "You're raising children and preaching to them to make a plan for their lives. But do you have one for yourself?" His response was eye opening: "I don't need you talking to me like this too." All my emotional blinders were gone, and I was back to acting fully based on logic. I was late to the conversation, but I had arrived in time to dodge the bullet! While I waited for my connecting flight, I contacted my assistant and filled her in. And thank sweet baby Jesus for my assistant, because she had returned all the gifts he had sent me by the time I arrived home.

Telling it now, this story sounds like an awkward moment in a buddy comedy, but back then it hit me hard. This pain was so deep that I became depressed. I lost my focus. This was one of my biggest dating failures, but once I was able to step back and analyze it, I realized it had been a blessing in disguise, bringing countless lessons and endless gratitude. Before this moment, I hadn't really stopped to think about my pillars, my standards, or how to go about attracting a man of quality into my life. After this moment, Darlin', I got organized. As I began to reflect after this episode there was one thing I knew for sure: Mommy Warbucks I will not be! I have no desire to be anybody's sugar mama. There are a few things one does not cross: my children, my clients, and my money!

In our society, women are often judged for going after a man because of what his wallet has to offer. These women are given titles like "gold digger" or "sponge." The rest of us are angered that our fellow women would be so lacking in character because, in a way, they're bringing us all down with them. We judge women harshly when they go after men for their power, money, and status. Then, we wonder why these men stay single or date multiple women at a time. Of course, it's because they have been burned and choose to keep women at a distance.

But how do we view it when the roles are reversed? How do we feel about "gold digging" men or the women they victimize? Men of character are equally outraged, if not more so, at the boys who treat women this way. But other boys are watching and taking notes. Sometimes we hear about a poor, lonely woman being conned out of her entire savings. It may not always be at that scale, but men take advantage of their partners' money all the time— just as often as women con men—but they aren't judged as harshly for it. The conversations I have had with women are shocking, yet their stories are rarely told. Likely because the women who fall victim to the cons are judged as naïve, stupid, or weak. Just look at the movies *Dirty Rotten Scoundrels* or *Shadow of a Doubt* for some classic examples of the charming con artist taking advantage of the naïve woman. (At least in *Dirty Rotten Scoundrels*, the tables are turned in the end.)

Pay close attention to this pillar: a man should be financially responsible if he wants to date a PowerWoman. Doesn't this sound simple? Doesn't this sound like a no-brainer? But financial stability can mean so many things to so many people. For some, it may have to do with sheer amount of money in a man's bank account, though in reality financial stability isn't about wealth—it's about how someone handles whatever amount of money they have. For me, the most important factor of my own financial stability is that I protect my children by protecting my money. I've learned this lesson the long, hard way. Pay attention to the choices prospective partners make with money and the conversations you have with them about finances. Ask the tough questions in the beginning.

Financial stability is not something to "work on" or figure out later with someone you are dating. If a man ever asks you for money for any other reason than he forgot his wallet, you need to cut him! I'm not saying the man needs to pay for everything in the relationship. It is fine to go Dutch or for you to pay sometimes— especially if you invited him on the date. But if a man starts to ask you to spot him for his bills or loan him money, cut him, no matter how long you have been dating him! Are you his mother or his girlfriend? These lessons aren't always easy to learn. It's been a challenge for me to look for a partner who brings clarity about and respect for money to the table, rather than the simple desire to dig into my pocketbook.

What I have learned about women and money is that learning to take care of our money is like learning to take care of ourselves. Meaning, we're often terrible at it—at least, at first. It is our nature to take care of loved ones first, business second, and ourselves last, and it's easy to let that tendency impact the way we protect (or don't protect) our money. When we are high-level givers, we must learn to guard against manipulation. The first step is simply being cognizant of how much money is coming in versus how much is going out—and where it's going. If you have a firm grasp on your earnings and your expenses, then you gain your power, lower your anxiety, and raise your standards for the men you date! This is dating wealth!

LESSONS OF A SINGLE MOM

What this man didn't realize was that, by asking me for money, he was asking me to take money away from my children to give to him. As PowerMoms, we work hard, sacrifice, and provide for our children. So, gentlemen, do not dare ask for money that our children need! When women start to look at our money in the sense of what it can do for our children, it becomes much easier to quit giving it to men who do not love us. If he asks for your money, he only loves your money—not you and definitely not your children!

When you are a PowerMom in the Singlehood, your money is much more than a vacation fund and a mortgage. We have college tuition, weddings, cars, and private school tuition to pay for, and the list grows as the children get older and the bills add up! When you fuck with a PowerMom's money, you are fucking with her children. So, how important is it that you provide for your children, and are you willing to let someone else control or jeopardize that? We work hard for our children, and we sacrifice a lot in order to give them more in life. To have someone ask for our money is a deep violation.

HOW TO SPOT POTENTIAL PROBLEMS

Back when I'd first entered the Singlehood, within a month of my divorce, a boy asked me to dinner. He had built and sold a company, he was very smart, and he seemed to be a great guy. Since this would be our first time meeting face-to-face, we were meeting at the restaurant. He asked me to stop by his brother's house to pick up something for him. His brother lived in my neighborhood, so logistically, this made sense, and I was happy to help. I did, and it was an envelope. I took it without much thought and headed on to the restaurant for my first Match.com date. Unfortunately, this was also my first experience being "catfished." Dude had used profile pictures that were at least ten years old! And that wasn't his only lie. Dinner just got more and more painful as I learned he was living with his cousin, he had driven his cousin's car to dinner, and, oh yes, he was unemployed. I guess I can give him a little credit for coming clean with his truth once we were face-to-face, but still, too little too late. I was naïve enough in the dating world back then that I felt terrible. I found myself wanting to pay for dinner to help the boy out. I didn't know what to do, and there was nothing to discuss except the fact that he had completely lied about everything, starting with his pictures! I was in shock! Then all the dude could say was, "You are so beautiful!" I had to go to the bathroom. I needed a break! When I returned, the bill had just arrived, and he was pulling the envelope I had gotten from his brother out of his pocket. It was cash, and he was using it to pay for dinner. Are you kidding me?! His *brother* was paying for our dinner. That's it! We are done! Bye, boy, bye! I thanked him for dinner and politely left. Groceries aside, there should never be a second date with a man in this condition.

You must discern your financial standards for men you consider dating. Do you need a man to have a good credit score? Do you need a man to be able to buy a house or at least make a house payment? Do you need him to have a retirement account? Or are you ok with him living with you—no job, no car, and every excuse in the world to protect the status quo? I've found my standards through trial and error.

How can you tell if a man meets your financial security standards? Sometimes it's very obvious, and sometimes it can take a while to discern because people can hide their financial savvy (or lack thereof) well. But, as with most of our standards, there are some telling signs that should cause you to take a closer look.

When you discover a man is living with family members or roommates, it's important to figure out why. Of course, there are many reasons to have a roommate, and maybe he's making a strategic choice to save money in order to achieve his next goals. The key, though, is to understand that financial motivation and be clear that (a) he's got a plan and (b) he's working toward realizing that plan. If, however, his story doesn't involve a plan for the future—if he says he's helping his mom or brother while they are in a tough spot but it's unclear what role he's playing, or if he can't articulate any aspirations about where he'd like to live next—watch out. It's likely this is a cover for financial instability, and the roommate or family is helping him pay the bills. We can't always judge a man by who he lives with, because there are reasons for everything and exceptions to every rule. But we can—and should—ask questions. What is important is whether his financial motivation is in alignment with you and your future.

Roommate situation aside, his housing can also be very telling. It is always very interesting to see a man renting an apartment while driving a Mercedes. I have seen this breed a lot in my years selling real estate! If a man in his 40s or 50s does not own a home, there is a reason, and it is almost always a red flag. You need to find out why he cannot commit to this investment. If you live in an unaffordable market, then what is his twenty-year plan? I met a man who needed to sell his home. He was a big talker, and he drove luxury vehicles, but he was planning to live in an apartment after the sale. This is unusual because, except under extenuating circumstances, most people who sell their homes purchase new ones. I sold his house with no problem, and I always declined his dinner invitations because I have a rule to never date a client. As it turns out, that rule helped me dodge a bullet. We got to the closing table, and the title officer requested the back child support payments he owed, along with the fees and interest that had accrued as he'd missed payments. I sat in silence as it all became clear. Needless to say, we never went out.

I've met many men who carry a lot of debt from divorce or poor spending habits. Debt in and of itself isn't necessarily bad— God knows sometimes we have to go into debt in order to take the next step up, such as buying a home or continuing our education. So while it's important to understand the source and extent of a man's debt, it's even more important to pay attention to what he is doing about it. Does he still spend money like he just won the lottery, or is he taking care to live within his means? Is he forthcoming about his financial situation, or does he try to hide it?

Women have married men only to learn they are carrying crippling debt after they say, "I do." I know women who have dated men for months, assuming they were financially stable, only to be blindsided when hidden debt has come to light after they got engaged or when the men have asked for tens of thousands of dollars to pay off a loan. Boys, do not mistake us for fools. When we learn the facts, we will get ahold of our emotions and you will lose us. It will hurt us, because we have been manipulated, but we'll make the hard choices.

I'll end this section with some basic advice: if you're dating somebody who uses the phrase "I forgot my wallet" more than once, cut him.

> *What is financial security to you?*
> *Are you asking hard financial questions?*
> *Are you willing to pay off a man's debt when/if*
> *you marry him?*
> *When you pay close attention, what patterns clue you in to*
> *a man's financial responsibility?*

WHO PAYS, AND FOR WHAT?

I'll never forget the incredibly good looking, financially stable man who owned his own business, traveled extensively, and who, despite being much younger than me, chased me for years. He asked me to catch a bite to eat at a casual restaurant, and I finally said yes. My meal was seven dollars, and he didn't offer to pay. Really? I mean, he had asked me to dinner! (Multiple times!) He'd discussed how well his business was doing, and then he didn't buy my seven-dollar dinner! Thank goodness we'd driven separately. He continued to call and text, but I never went out with him again. I am worth a whole lot more than seven dollars! There are people who take me to lunch just for my business advice, and they pay more than seven dollars!

Ladies, if a man is not willing to take you out and buy your dinner, he is not worth your time. (On the flip side, if you are not financially stable enough to take a man out and buy his dinner, then you may need to work on yourself too!) I'm not saying he has to be able to buy you a three-course steak dinner on the regular, but too many women settle and make excuses for men who are unable—or worse, able but unwilling—to take them out at all! If you just want someone to go to dinner with, that's what girlfriends are for. Set your standards! Remember how we talked about your hourly rate? Keep that in mind, and let it influence your expectations of the men you date. Do you expect them to take you to McDonalds or a five star restaurant? Do you expect them to pay, go Dutch, or ask you to pay? That may be a date-by-date question, but it's still a question worth thinking about. I have found that men appreciate it if you offer to split the bill. They will let you know their expectations once you offer. If they expect you to pay for the entire bill on the first date, cut them! That's not a date—that is a boy whose mother got the night off from cooking.

What about expenses other than meals? What about travel— is it always as unwise as my trip to Europe? No, ma'am! I had a conversation recently with a beautiful woman in her early

20s who had met a man on a recent trip to California. Now he wanted to come visit her, but she was hesitant, and she was asking me for advice. Here's my advice, ladies: if a man is willing to come visit you, let that lovin' fly in to visit! If a man is willing to fly you to meet him, let him! Let lovin' experience a new place! If a man wants you and sees your value, he will make it happen, and airfare or a road trip will be minimal and won't stand in his way. That said, you should *always* have an escape plan when you travel. For example, I previously went with a boy who was really good looking and we had potential for a future until he moved out of state. We kept in touch on and off until he reached out saying he was desperate to see me. I bought a plane ticket, but he cancelled the day before I was to fly out. Don't invest real money in a relationship unless you know for a fact that it's a safe investment.

How do you and your partners determine
who pays on a date?
How often do you expect your man to foot the bill?
How does your hourly rate influence your financial
standards for a partner?

CHECKING FOR FINANCIAL VALUES ALIGNMENT

I have friends who have fallen in love and married only to realize the financial balance was not what they had expected. Their spending habits weren't aligned with each other's (or, in some cases, with their means), or their expectations of whether they would assume each other's financial responsibility were out of sync. These things are important to consider early in a relationship. Do your financial philosophies match up? As things get serious, are you going to be expected to assume part of his education debt or support his children as well as yours?

A mutual friend set me up with a much older man, and the age difference introduced a new financial concern: retirement. What did his retirement plan look like? Was he prepared, or was I going to be supporting him? How did he expect to spend his retirement? In an RV, in rocking chairs on the front porch, or traveling the world on a jet plane? It was a new perspective, and it was so important. I asked questions about his retirement savings and picked apart his twenty-year plan on the first date. He had everything figured out financially, and while the age difference was too much for me in the end, the new perspective I'd gained from talking with him taught me so much.

When you know where every penny goes and how it grows, you'll be able to speak with power in every area of your life, checking for alignment with potential partners *before* you encounter any nasty financial surprises. The old standard we have been programmed with is to let men manage the finances in a relationship. But if we fail to pay attention to money because of these stereotypical roles, we're liable to find ourselves very unhappy in mismatched partnerships. In order to get clear on whether your potential partner's financial values are aligned with yours, you need to be clear on what your money does for you. I know what my five-, ten-, and twenty-year plans look like, which empowers me to have in-depth conversations about finances on a first date. If our values are not in alignment, there is no need to go out on a second date—it would be a waste of my time, which is also a waste of my money.

LADIES, STAY IN CONTROL OF YOUR MONEY

When it comes to money management, we have been doing a disservice to the younger generation of women. CNBC discovered that studies are showing a backward trend in financial decision-making in relationships with those between the ages of 20 to 34.[37] Women in this age range are deferring major financial decisions to their significant others and not staying present or involved in their joint finances. Is this 2020 or 1920? Darlin', you may be busy, in love, trusting, or maybe even a little fearful, but you have got to get your hands messy in the money, honey! The unforeseen happens in life all the time, and there is no guarantee your significant other will be here tomorrow. Are you prepared to pay the bills, contribute to the savings accounts, meet with the attorneys, and take full control of your life if your husband disappears? I was the breadwinner in my family when I divorced, but when it came to finances, I had put my head in the sand and let my husband take the reins. I had not paid a bill in over fifteen years. I still wrote checks, despite the existence of online banking! What was a ROTH, a SEP, or a 529? I had no idea! Please, do better than I did. You're a PowerWoman, and that means having power over your money!

When it comes to combining finances, I suggest you keep your money separate! Especially when you're dating, and maybe even when you get married. You earned it—it's yours! This does not mean a man who makes less than you cannot be your fit, or visa-versa, but it means you should always have the final say in what you do with the money *you earned*. And so should he with his money. Everyone should be involved in the finances, contribute to the joint bills, and stay aware of the individual and collective financial situations. But keeping your money separate ensures you're free to live the life you want to live. For one thing, when you have control over your finances, it means you have an escape plan. If things go south, you can leave without worrying about money. But even when things are going well, use that money to take fabulous vacations on your own and with your girlfriends! Do the things that fulfill you—and use your own money to do them so that you're never reliant on a man for your next plane ticket or adventure. Live life to the fullest, on your own terms, and always ask a lot of questions—especially when it comes to money!

Evaluating another's financial stability takes time, vulnerability, presence, and transparency, but most importantly, it starts with being confident in how you define *your* relationship with money and finances. If you don't know yet, it's time to figure it out! And don't be afraid to ask for help. It's ok to say, "I need help in order to gain clarity and power with my money." It's the same as walking into the salon and saying, "Someone help me with these roots!" What if we prioritized money as much as we prioritized our hair? In her *Women and Money* podcast episode called "The Money Mind," Suze Orman says, "Money is the physical manifestation of who you are."[38] Our money says so much about us, and it's important that we're intentional about how we reflect that with a partner.

What does your relationship to money say about you?
What does a partnership look like regarding
finances to you?
Have you been held back in relationships due to how you
define yourself or others with money?

Choose Me!

I had sold a house to a buyer, and when I went to the home inspection, the seller was home. He happened to be a single man, and five days later, he asked me to dinner. He was a single dad, we both had rigorous schedules, our custody arrangements were the complete opposite, and I lived in the city while he lived in the suburbs. The only times we had available to see each other for weeks were over lunch and coffee dates. Yet despite all of these hurdles—not to mention the fact that he was packing and moving out of the house I'd just sold—this man made time for me. He *chose* me.

Unfortunately, there were other hurdles in his world that kept us out of alignment, but dating him was a fantastic reminder that a man will always show how he will prioritize you, especially in the beginning of a relationship. If he doesn't prioritize you in the beginning, when he should be putting his very best foot forward, what makes you think he'll prioritize you once he's comfortable? What I know for sure is that people do what they want to do, and they find time and make time for the people they want to spend time with. When a man sees value in you, he will make time for you. If a man does not make time for you, then you are not a priority. And if a man isn't smart enough to make you a priority, why would you waste any of your time on him?

But choosing you isn't only about making time. It's also about attention and consideration for your interests and goals and preferences. Does he suggest the same kind of cuisine even though you've said you're not a big fan? Does he stay in touch when you're not together? Does he try the things you like to do? Does he take initiative with you in small and big ways? Or does he expect you to be his Runaway Bride, subverting your authentic self to make the relationship about him and his interests and desires?

As with all pillars, you get to decide what your expectations are, and you get to uphold your standard. But first, you have to decide what that standard is and learn to spot the signs of whether you're aligned or not. How does he choose to provide for you? And I don't mean financially. I mean, how does he make time for you? How does he scratch your itches? How curious is he about you, your experiences, and what makes you tick?

Ladies, keep in mind that this pillar is a two-way street: if you see value in a partner, you have to make him a priority as well. I may work sixteen-hour days, but I will make time for you if I see potential in you and our relationship. If we don't choose them, we can't expect them to choose us. Part of setting that standard, though, requires us to reciprocate.

I am close with a single PowerMan who has been in a long-distance relationship for several years, and it fascinates me! For years, he and a woman have lived in separate states and chosen each other consistently. They do not limit themselves based on geography, and they provide companionship in each other's worlds. To be very clear, each of them are amazing people in every pillar and both are raising and prioritizing children. Yet they have also fine-tuned the art of choosing one another in this way until the next season of life allows them to choose one another under the same roof. They choose each other, make time for one another, vacation with one another, and fulfill one another without limits.

LESSONS OF A SINGLE MOM

As moms, we're so accustomed to taking care of our families that it's easy to fall into the trap of subverting our own needs and desires to prioritize others. It may be tempting to settle for someone who doesn't make us a priority, either because we're used to being the one driving our relationships or because we just like having somebody "grown up" to spend time with. As mothers, we forget to put on our own oxygen masks, and we forget what it looks like for someone to prioritize us, because we are no longer prioritizing ourselves. The more we learn to put ourselves first, the more firmly we'll be able to establish that standard for the men in our lives as well. [End box]

WHAT DOES CHOOSING LOOK LIKE TO YOU?

I was dating a man who came across as a really "good" man. He came from a well-respected family in town, attended church every Sunday, had an impressive occupation, and was a very involved father of his children. And, wow, was he hot! We talked about church, children, and interests, and we laughed a lot. What was not to like? Our first dates were in group settings, so deeper conversations were limited. But something didn't feel right. He was too smooth.

One Friday night, he messaged me to cancel our plans, saying that he unexpectedly had his kids, which I certainly understood. Later, he sent SnapChat photos of him getting ready for bed. SnapChat qualms aside, the photos were cute! That night, I went to a late dinner with some girlfriends, and afterward I wanted to stay out, so I messaged a guy friend from high school who was a rounder. He literally traveled the country to party! I knew if I called him, he would be up for a night on the town, and sure enough, he was on board. We headed to the club.

And who was there, standing at the bar with a much younger woman dancing around him? Mr. Sleepytown, himself. He certainly wasn't spending time with his children, like he'd said. He saw me across the room and almost dropped his drink. The next week at the salon, I found out that not only he had been dating this girl longer than he had been with me, but he was also seeing other women. I could have saved myself a lot of time and effort by getting my hair done sooner!

First and foremost, I'm not going to date somebody who lies to me. But even if he hadn't lied outright, he clearly wasn't choosing me at the level that I wanted to be chosen. We need to decide what being chosen looks like to us early on, especially in two areas: who initiates the relationship, and whether dating around is okay.

My standard may seem old-fashioned to many, but I believe the man should initiate the relationship. Why? I've seen a pattern in conversations with the people whose relationships I admire the most: when they met, the man pursued the woman every time. He asked for her number, he messaged her on social media, he asked her to dinner, he called or texted her initially, and he courted her. The pattern I was learning was to not seek a man but to allow him to seek me. The only way for this to happen was to become content with where I was and who I was. I had to become very comfortable with being single, not needing a relationship, and falling out of love with being in love. And, as I've mentioned, I needed to learn never to chase a man. Only then, I decided, would the right man seek me. This mentality took years to develop as I continued to fail in the dating space. The men whose profiles online and on dating apps indicated they were looking for a successful and intellectual woman—the men I so wanted to choose me—would disappear after a few conversations, as though they were scared of me.

In her book *The Love Gap*, Jenna Birch validates the pattern I was experiencing with her research. She discovered that when women become the more successful parties and the breadwinners in relationships, men tend to feel emasculated. They prefer not to date unless they feel as if they can be the provider in the relationship. In other words, men weren't choosing me because they didn't feel they brought enough to the table. It seemed I was going to be single forever if I didn't convince them otherwise! I was often tempted to break my own rule, chasing these men myself. But my experiences doing just that told me that, at least in my dating life, it wasn't a wise option. The right man wouldn't need to be convinced. It was so telling when I went out with a man who listened to me describe my journey and then said, "Wow. I have to decide if I'm ok with being Mr. Claire Brown." Next!

That night, after the divorce was finalized, when the girls took me to the club, a man asked me for my phone number and for a dinner date the following week. We exchanged numbers, but I didn't hear from him for four days. Keep in mind that the last time I had been single was during the days of landlines and answering machines. I didn't know who was supposed to text who, who called who, or whether email was even an option. (As a side note, after being in the Singlehood for about six months with countless disappointments and massive confusion about dating technology, I decided to empower myself to dominate the dating space by reading all the dating books. After all, this was how I had solved problems in other areas of life. *He's Just Not That Into You* by Greg Behrendt and Liz Tuccillo rocked my world!) Anyway, I had his number, so I decided to call and find out if we were still going to dinner. When I called, it was obvious he was not alone, and we were not going to dinner that week or ever! I quickly learned that, if a man is interested, he'll show you before you have time to wonder. If he doesn't call, send a text, e-mail, or carrier pigeon, or otherwise pursue you in some fashion, then he is just not that into you!

When I stopped chasing men, I found clarity in myself, and men of worth and quality began to find me. I realized I no longer needed an app or a website to find affirmation. This looks different for everyone, but for me it meant no longer actively seeking a partner or being the initiator in a relationship. Instead, I started resting in my own happiness in the Singlehood. When I settled into my happiness, men started to show up in my world without effort. There were options, and I was doing the choosing, which brings me to question number two: is it okay to date around in a relationship? Well, that depends on what you're comfortable with, but here's my perspective. First of all, until one man rises to the top and you're ready to enter a committed relationship, why would you *not* date more than one suitor? That doesn't mean you have to have sex with all of them or get serious with all of them, but "playing the field" gives you a good opportunity to get to know a wide variety of potential partners and see for yourself what you want and don't want in a man. A wonderful single girlfriend recently dated two men for almost six months. This gave her time to discover who was aligned with her standards so she could be confident in her choice. Why not have brother husbands?

That said, it's also important to make your expectations about monogamy versus dating around very clear. Don't let him think you're exclusive yet if that's not your plan. If you're dating around and seeing other people, then it's likely that he will too. If you're not comfortable with that, you'll need to examine whether you really want to be dating around yourself. If and when you decide you want him to be yours and you want to be taken off the market, then you must have the DTR conversation—define the relationship! If he wants you, he will be on board! The timing of this conversation is different for each of us. I know many women who have wanted exclusivity after two weeks of dating and others who have waited six months. When to have the DTR conversation depends on your own personal boundaries and preferences. How well do you share with others? Are you comfortable having sex with someone who is also seeing and sleeping with others? Is he having the DTR conversation with you before he tries to initiate sex?

A man will show you pretty quickly how committed he is and how he wants to be there for you. Is he with you when it is convenient for him, or is he with you when you are available? If he's not prioritizing you, don't waste your time, because the right man deserves more of your time right now! I don't know about you, but I want a man who desires me as much as I desire him. Wouldn't it be great to have that teenage love again, where you can't stop thinking about him, you're constantly planning little things to surprise him and make him happy, and you get giddy when he calls and texts? He should feel the same desire and excitement about you!

When a man truly sees you—all of you—he will move mountain ranges to fit into your world. As PowerWomen, we are extremely focused on our purpose and our priorities, neither of which include "snagging a man!" There's no time to wedge ourselves in where we don't fit and aren't valued. Instead, we have to look for partners who are eager to make space for us in their worlds—and for whom we're eager to do the same. Remain focused, and soon you'll find yourself with plenty of choices!

How can you tell if a man is prioritizing you?
How do you show a man you're prioritizing him?
Have you settled in the past for men who wouldn't or
didn't choose you?
Would you prefer to pursue or be pursued?
How do you set boundaries for dating around
versus exclusivity?

IS HE STILL CHOOSING AN EX?

I had been dating a man exclusively for about three months when we had a discussion about money and he disclosed that he was still managing his ex-wife's finances even though they had been divorced for over two years. Here is how this conversation went:

Dude: She's dealing with a lot, and I'm still helping her do

DATING PILLAR: CHOOSE ME!

the online banking and managing the bills.

Me: When you were married did you also manage the finances and not have sex?

Dude: Well, yeah.

Me: So, is the only difference between being married and divorced the fact that you live in separate houses?

Next please!

If a man is still in charge of his ex-wife's expenses, daily affairs, car maintenance, or shopping excursions, there is an issue. Do not date this man. He is an enabler, and you will find yourself raising two adult children: the man and the ex-wife! Ain't nobody got time for that! Not all marriages are the same, and neither are divorces. Some men continue to coddle their ex-wives, but this is so unhealthy for everyone involved, and it precludes him from truly choosing you. After all, anyone who shares children and finances is basically married in today's society because, let's get real, most *married* couples don't share much more than children and finances! There are many, many really good men in our society who are technically divorced and still emotionally or financially supporting their exes beyond what is required in their divorce decrees. These men are not ready for you.

Early in my dating journey, a woman who is much older than me told me, "If he doesn't shut up about his ex, then run as fast as you can!" At the time, I hadn't encountered a man like this, and I laughed it off. But a couple of years later, it seemed every man who came across my path for several months wanted to discuss his ex-wife, his past relationships, or his divorce endlessly. I found myself being in the friend-zone—and sometimes even in the therapist seat—with some of these guys. It turned out my girlfriend's advice was wise! While it's healthy to discuss prior relationships in order to gauge each other's patterns and growth, entire dates should not revolve around those topics. When a man is fixated on an ex or his divorce, he hasn't healed. Are they friends, or is he filled with venom?

This became very clear when a very close friend in town went through a very public divorce. While he was married, we would go to lunch about once a quarter to discuss different business ideas and topics. Now that he's divorced, and we're both single adults in our small-town fish bubble, we've dropped the public lunches to avoid gossip. But we've still managed to maintain a friendship and find enlightening business conversation on our own terms. Recently, I reached out for business advice, and he kept moving the conversation to his divorce, his ex-wife, and how he was choosing to not date. What I learned is that when we are not healed from a painful relationship, it becomes the topic of all our conversations, romantic or otherwise. No matter how hard we may try, we will not be able to hide trauma or pain. When someone shows you they aren't over their ex by always making them the topic of conversation, believe them. They are not choosing you because they aren't able to yet. Run!

Here's an extreme example: there is nothing better than the man who will blatantly tell you he is going back for "seconds" all the time with his ex-wife! There is an incredibly hot, successful, and financially responsible man who I have known for many, many years. He is an amazing father and a man of faith. And he's single—sometimes. He and I have referred business to one another for years, and many times the conversation has turned to dating. We have flirted heavily, but we've never gone out, largely because he readily discloses that though they will never remarry, he continues to see his ex-wife. Out of curiosity, I asked him why he got divorced and why he keeps going back. Clarity is so interesting sometimes. He said, "I don't want the work of the chase, and it's a good piece of ass. So, it works." His answer validated the findings from the Good Men Project as to why many men stay married and why many try to get back with their exes after the divorce.[39] In short: they're lazy. There are three things I know for sure: comfortability and mediocrity will never lead to a healthy and growing relationship, that ass won't always be hot, and this man is not ready to prioritize anyone else!

Darlin', if he's constantly talking about her, if he still manages her finances, if he doesn't introduce you to mutual friends of the ex, and especially if he's still sleeping with her, too, then he is still married for all practical purposes, and he is still choosing his ex-wife. And if that's the case, choosing him ain't worth your time. Know your worth, and if he's a match, he will see it clearly enough to prune the branches and choose you.

WHAT SIGNALS ARE YOU SENDING WHEN YOU RESPOND?

Remember how I said engagements and proposals peak on social media during the holidays? Something about the fall and winter months just makes the boys want to cuddle up. The inventory of choices in your dating apps will increase at this time of the year.

Another prime time in the Singlehood is mid-spring. See, many people wait until the holidays are over to file for divorce. The University of Washington did a study about the seasonal filings for divorce, and they found filings flood in beginning in January and peak in March.[40] The couple gets through the holidays "for the kids" or whatever other excuse they can come up with not to spoil Christmas. Then, January, February, and March are filled with divorce filings. Those divorces are finalized in March through May, and as that happens, fresh meat hits the market! I'm always telling you to pay attention to patterns, and this one's no exception: if you are discouraged with dating, remember that spring is coming!

But when your inbox is flooded with requests from newly single men, be careful how you respond, because you're likely sending a signal. A man so new to the Singlehood is likely still hung up on his ex and not ready to choose anybody yet. When you ignore that and let him in anyway, you're saying that you're okay not being a priority.

In fact, the way we women respond to men in any situation matters, as our responses to their invitations or outreach set the tone for how we are to be treated. Are you to be taken to nice restaurants that require him to make reservations in advance, or are you a last-minute "booty call" kind of girl? You tell him based on which of his phone calls and texts you answer. Remember that you are a woman of worth. If he's worthy of you, he has no other choice than to choose you by making time for you and by planning ahead to be sure he can get on your calendar. After all, you are the hottest ticket in town, and he would be crazy to not prioritize you! Make this your mindset. If you don't, why would he? You set the expectations for how you are to be courted based on how you respond to his invitations. Are you only making yourself available for lunch and coffee dates? Are you requiring prospects to plan ahead and make a reservation if they want to take you to dinner? Or are you sending the message that you'll settle for impromptu late-night "Netflix and chill" sessions by responding to his ten o'clock texts?

We also need to be careful how we respond when we sense a man is reaching out because he's lonely. I've dated amazing men who live out of state, and some of them continually circle back around. Why is this? What I know for sure is that we all get lonely, and I suspect this is why these long-distance men get back in touch. Many boys will reach out this way, so beware! If he doesn't make an effort to maintain a real relationship—courting you and coming see you—then he is not interested or worth your time. He's simply looking for a pen pal when he starts to get stuck in the Lonely. And while we can certainly sympathize, it's not in our best interest to encourage this behavior or mistake it for courtship. He is dealing with some other issues that he needs to work out.

When you're considering how to respond to an invitation, the first pattern to look for is how he typically reaches out to you. Does he communicate with you regularly? Does he wait until late in the week to make weekend plans? When does he text or call? You can tell a lot about his priorities—and whether you're one of them—by looking at this pattern. Next, when and how are you choosing to respond to his invitations? The guy that calls on a Friday and asks me to go to dinner that night is going to be disappointed. My mother can't even get on my calendar that quick unless it's an emergency! If you are always rearranging your schedule and making yourself available for him and his needs, then you're teaching him that he doesn't have to prioritize you, because you'll be there when it's convenient for him. If that's the message you send when you respond to his last-minute invitations, how will you show him how valuable your time is and how valuable *you* are? A man will prioritize you as much as you prioritize yourself. It's very important to remember that we have choices in every scenario in life. We may not always *like* our choices, but we still have them. If someone expects us to be constantly available, it is because we have chosen to be that way for them.

How do you choose to respond to last-minute invitations
from men you date?
How do you use your responses to show men
how much you value your time?

ARE YOU CHOOSING YOU?

Mark Manson, the author of the huge hit, *The Subtle Art of Not Giving a F*ck*, decided to crowdsource the ultimate relationship guide by polling his hundreds of thousands of followers for advice and boiling the responses down to twelve core ideas from 1,500 people in the most satisfying relationships.[41] One of my favorite points in the guide is that a "healthy and happy relationship requires two healthy and happy individuals. ... Two people with their *own* identities, their *own* interests and perspectives, and things they do *by themselves*, on their *own* time."

He also reminds us that these individuals must not only prioritize each other, but also prioritize themselves. "A relationship based on constant and mutual sacrifices can't be sustained and will eventually become damaging to both individuals."

When I entered the Singlehood at age 34, I quickly realized how little I'd been prioritizing myself. I've already told you how deep I fell into the Lonely and how lost I felt. That was because I had built my identity around my husband and children and lost myself in my family's needs, preferences, and schedules. I was on the verge of repeating that pattern with the men I started dating early in my singlehood journey. Do you have the friend who is at every event until she gets a boyfriend? Then her preferences, her schedule, and her entire life suddenly revolve around the boyfriend. If you are lucky enough to schedule plans she will inevitably cancel for more time with, you guessed it, the boyfriend. We all know these people, and we all swear we won't become these people. But when we don't create a foundation as healthy individuals, we are more likely to fall into that trap. When you choose yourself, you can let someone else add layers and depth and richness to your life, but they don't define who you are.

Psychology Today calls this the "Unselfish Art of Prioritizing Yourself."[42] By choosing yourself as a priority, you are refueling yourself to be able to choose others. If your partner loves Nascar racing, and you choose him by watching all things Nascar, attending Nascar events, and learning all things Nascar but do not take time to do something you love and enjoy just as much, then you will become resentful not of only Nascar but of your partner. Choosing yourself and what you enjoy is a key part of both self-care and relationship maintenance. If you enjoy marathon running, then go have that experience in order to fulfill yourself. Then you'll both be able to bring passion and enthusiasm to the table as you discuss each other's pursuits. Just because you are partners does not mean you must do everything together. It's healthier to have separate interests that you support one another in, as well as common interests.

How do you balance your interests with your partner's?
What passions have you set aside that you'd like to
bring back into your life?

How are you choosing to fulfill yourself as a person,
woman, mother, and partner?

Another important piece of choosing yourself is building your tribe: nurturing a community of friends, independent of your relationship, that lifts you up, sets you straight when needed, and brings another dimension of joy and love to your life. I learned this the hard way, too, when I entered the Singlehood. I didn't know any other single women my age. I no longer felt like I fit in my regular circles because I carried shame from divorce. People I had thought were friends abandoned me, and friends in the trenches of life were busy keeping their own marriages together. As human beings, we need a sense of belonging. It is even on Maslow's hierarchy of needs. But I had based my entire sense of belonging on my husband, and now that he was out of the picture, I quickly found myself in need of a strong support system of women. I needed girlfriends to go to lunch and dinner and on trips with. I needed girlfriends to go out with, to share in escapades that would leave us giggling for days. I wasn't choosing myself at a high level, and it took becoming uncomfortable to recognize the largest needs in my life.

If I had been going on trips with girlfriends, a trip to Europe with the wrong boy wouldn't have been so appealing. If I had stronger relationships with women in my life, then I would be more fulfilled within myself and not so apt to fall in love with sweet rhetoric from a man. If I had stronger friendships in my life, then I wouldn't be so quick to jump into relationships. Even as I began to develop and nurture my own passions, this community was the missing piece preventing me from loving myself wholeheartedly like Mother Brené discusses. This was me choosing myself!

As in most scenarios, when I recognized my need, I took action. I contacted some moms who I considered to be intellectual, authentic, and all fun as hell. We became PowerMoms, and that meant leveraging one another as we rise in all areas of life. I discovered love and support that every woman should experience, married or single, mother or not. I had to share this kind of community, and it became my purpose. (Even though these incredible women have yet to manage to set me up on a decent date with anyone!)

LESSONS OF A SINGLE MOM

As parents we start to play rock-paper-scissors to see who gets to go to the grocery store in order to have alone time. We find ourselves hiding in the closet to talk on the phone so we can have a quiet conversation away from our children. If you are in the early years of parenting, to go a day without spit-up or poop somewhere on your clothing is a miracle. My married friends envy the alone time I have without my children, and I crave the time they have with theirs. When everything revolves around the kids, how are you fulfilling *yourself* in the middle of your parenting phase? How are you still maintaining the space to allow yourself to dream? What is something you are trying each year that is new, exciting, and brings joy to only you?

As your promising dates turn into committed relationships that may even be headed toward marriage, you'll both work to continue to choose each other and make the relationship a partnership. You will make each other a priority because you truly respect one another. He will become your person, your best friend, and your love, and that is irreplaceable. It is ok to take off the armor and let this in. But remember, many men will choose you. Which one *you* choose is up to you, and you'll be prepared to make the strongest choice if you've learned to choose yourself first.

Dating from the Carpool Lane

There is a fabulous quote from the movie *Jerry McGuire*, in which Rod Tidwell gives Jerry advice about dating a single mom: "I feel for you, man. But a real man wouldn't shoplift the pootie from a single mom."

What women will not freely admit to the men they are dating is that when she gives up the pootie, she's almost always in it for the long haul. But single moms? When they give up the pootie, you can bet they are seeing a future together, and this future absolutely includes their children. Consequently, a real man won't "shoplift the pootie of a single mom"—he won't mess around with a single mom if he's not interested in anything more than a fling. Or, at least, he'll be honest about exactly what he's looking for so that she knows the score before making her choices.

But making our kids a priority in our lives, especially in our dating lives, is about more than just having or not having sex. A real man who chooses to date a single mom won't shoplift her time, her attention, or her efforts to make her kids feel like a priority either. When a man chooses to date a PowerMom, he understands that he is also dating her children, whether he ever meets them or not.

It's on us, as single moms, to discern the real men from the shoplifters and to make it clear that we won't allow anybody to distract us from our children. My love for my children is so deep that I strive to provide them with the best I can give them. So why would I settle in any area of my life that affects them? I have always and will always make it very clear: my children came before and come before any other relationship in my life. The divorce was not their choice, but I made the choice to be a parent, and they will always be my priority. Does he encourage time with the children? How does he foster my relationship with my children? If he doesn't then he's not worth my time.

As a parent, do you notice how your children will quietly do their homework, play with their toys, or read their books...until you get on the phone? Somehow getting on the phone and paying attention to someone other than them will trigger a child's transformation into the demon you swore your child would never be! Attention seeking behavior in children is normal, so how do you think they respond when you start giving attention to a new partner?

Do you have a plan to help your child transition from mom to mom-plus-one?
How will you prepare them for the shift in attention?
How will you reassure them they are the priority?
Do your actions align with your message?

YOUR KIDS, YOUR PRIORITY

I had always wanted a house full of children. But early in my life, it became clear that that would be difficult for me. Surgeries, procedures, injections, hormones, and doctor appointments can take the joy out of the process, but I was determined to become a mother.

Finally, it happened. The joy of pregnancy after a fertility struggle was like nothing I've ever experienced. I was filled with gratitude, and an overwhelming sense of happiness oozed from me. In the second trimester, however, during a routine exam, the doctor discovered a tragedy. My belly had been growing, but the heartbeat inside had stopped.

There is no way to describe the pain of losing a child, but we persevered. More surgeries and more hormones later, I have two amazing children. After my son's delivery, though, I had to have a hysterectomy at age 30. The dream of more pitter-patter in my home disappeared right out of my vagina.

Knowing all this, you might understand how important my children are to me. But I don't believe that I'm special in that regard, or that I should be special. Every woman's journey into motherhood is personal, and we each make our own decisions in this space. Sometimes life makes them for us. When women who are dating continue to prioritize their children as the gifts from God that they are, they will raise their standards in all areas. We must treasure our gifts and do everything in our power to protect our children, prioritize them, and help them see that they are our number one. Your children need to know how much you value them and where they fit in your life, especially as they're dealing with the major life changes that come before, during, and after their parents' divorce.

You can read about the effects of divorce on a child for the rest of your life and never run out of material or research. Repeatedly, researchers find children of divorce feel a sense of abandonment.[43] As a child of divorce and now a divorcée, I can relate to what my children are experiencing. We all crave stability, acceptance, and love. We all have a need to feel important, be heard, and know that we matter. It's not always easy to provide that, but we can always try. Often, as adults, we are able to see transitions to come in the future. If we anticipate a change in custody schedule, one parent dating, or one parent getting remarried, we can prepare our children for these events to help them eliminate their anxiety and equip them with positive feelings. And along those lines, one of the best decisions I have ever made was to make my divorce work. We decided if we couldn't make the marriage work, we would make the divorce work, and we do. We choose to put our feelings for our children before our own, and we place the interest of our children first and foremost in every situation we encounter as co-parents. Our children are the priority, regardless of our marital status.

If you're a single mom, whether you're in a relationship or not, how are you protecting your children? How are you validating their feelings and reassuring them about the future? How are you being present with them? When your children seek your attention, how are you addressing their emotions and not the behavior, as *PsychCentral* suggests?[44]

In short, as single PowerMoms in the dating game, how are we to ensure our kids know they're still our top priorities?

First, if we're sharing custody, it helps to be honest with ourselves and others about the loneliness we feel when we're separated from our children. When you only see your children half the time, the Lonely is palpable. For me, it was the most difficult loneliness I had ever experienced. The source of my joy was gone for days at a time. The children I had desired all my life and fought a medical battle to conceive were now only with me half the time. The loss of my spouse was one pain, but not having my children every day seemed like a pit I couldn't climb out of at times.

We lose sight of how precious our time is with our children. We become weighted with sports, homework, meltdowns, and breastfeeding while juggling our careers, relationships, activity schedules, and lack of sleep. But when my kids went to their dad's house, all I wanted was to hear their voices on a daily basis, cuddle with them at night, sing to them at bedtime, and pack their lunches each day. Creating these opportunities became important. School field trips and surprise lunches at school became much more precious. I cherish our time to talk around the dinner table, or I insist we talk in the car instead of turning on the radio. But I still grieve not being physically present for all of life's precious moments. I will never get those moments back.

I know PowerMoms who only see their children twice a month, and not by their choosing. I know PowerMoms who have seven kids with them full-time while they run huge companies. We all have different journeys, and each of us battles the Lonely in a different way. But what remains true is, despite the desire for romantic companionship, we will always love our children above everything else! A PowerMom may be many things, but she will always be, first and foremost, a mother. It has truly been a gift to be single as long as I have, because I have been able to spend more time with my children and absorb them at a higher level.

How much is time with your children worth?
What does being present look like to you?
How are you making space in your life to
talk to your children?

There is no decision I make that does not impact my children in one way or another. Every success and every failure in my life has the potential to affect them. Your children may not be physically present at all times, but the choices you make as their PowerMom will still impact them at a high level. You will always be the voice in their head when they make decisions in life, and it's up to you to learn how to empower them to know that you are always present with them, regardless of your physical location. Maintaining individual time and dates with your children are key. Continually letting your children know how and why they are loved through conversations and by expressing yourself in their love languages will instill confidence in your children and strengthen your relationship with them.

Many times, as PowerMoms, we have expectations for our dating life that are not in alignment with our children's expectations. It's important to talk about those expectations so that children feel heard and know their feelings about potential relationships matter. My children and I maintain an ongoing and open conversation about dating—my dating life and, now, increasingly and unbelievably, theirs. With my son, that means discussing what a gentleman looks like, sharing examples of how men have shown that to me (or not), and listening to him talk about how he intends to be a gentleman to a lady one day. As my daughter now receives attention from boys, our conversations are becoming more and more frequent, and I feel the pressure! She and I also discuss how a gentleman should behave, but more importantly, we discuss a young PowerWoman's choices and behaviors.

As single PowerMoms, many of us feel pressure to provide a partner for our children as an example of a relationship, courtship, or even as a male role model. But the idea that we need a man around to teach our children is a limiting belief. We can accomplish everything we need on our own if we're willing to engage with our children. By playing the "gentleman game" with my son, having him point out men in public who are gentlemen, I help him see the model of a man and identify positive behavior to emulate. As you might imagine, this opens up multiple opportunities for conversations to reassure my children about themselves and their futures and to clarify that they are my priority.

How are you choosing to empower your children, their mindsets, and their behavior in all areas?
What conversations are you having with your children to help them recognize appropriate dating behaviors for the future?

THE WARNING SIGNS OF A SHOPLIFTER

Dating as a PowerMom is definitely an adventure! The schedule is tough. Availability is an issue. Attempts to talk on the phone when the children are awake are not pretty. Do you remember when you were growing up and your siblings would say things or make noises to embarrass you while you were on the phone with a boy? I don't know about your children, but my children have taken up the sibling role, making noises and silly comments with gusto. If a man respects you, he will wait to talk with you. If a man respects you, he will respect you even more because of how you prioritize your children. When a man asks about when you have your children, what time they go to bed, and whether it is ok to call according to the children's schedule, pay attention! He is a man of worth who values you, your time, and your children!

You are your children's protector and their comfort, and they should be your focus. Your children need to be made to feel as if they are always valued, and you can show this through your actions and through who you allow into your life.

So, how do you determine whether a man is the type who will prioritize your children and your time with them? Look for the PowerMan. The PowerMan will prioritize his children in the same way you prioritize yours. The PowerMan will be present with his children, and he will be very involved in their lives. Being in alignment in how you value parenting is so important, especially if the children still live at home. Does he inquire about your custody schedule? Does he make sure to not call or text during special times with your children, such as dinner and bedtime? Does he ask questions about your children and take an interest in their interests?

On the other hand, if a man is emotionally immature, he will be jealous of you, your children, and probably other relationships in your life. I have had many girlfriends cut men after just a couple of months when it became clear the men weren't willing to allow them to put their children first. Cancelled dates due to sick children or changes in the custody schedule come with the territory of dating a PowerMom, and a PowerMan will be understanding. (This makes it very important never to use your children as an excuse to get out of a date.) Children need support; adults just want it. There is a difference! The adults you bring into your life should be able to support themselves. If they can't, then they aren't emotionally mature.

There was a man who lived about an hour from me, and we had been to dinner once. It was nice enough, though he talked about his divorce far too much. He had asked me to brunch the following weekend, and I'd accepted. But the day before brunch, we had an unexpected change in our custody schedule, and I had to call to reschedule the date. Rather than understanding and accepting that I was going to put my children first, he cancelled altogether and followed up with text messages launching inappropriate accusations. You never know the baggage someone else is carrying. Make sure they have worked through it before you involve your children.

When a potential partner has children himself, how he treats them is a fantastic indicator of whether he'll ever be worthy of being part of your children's life. Does he create the same boundaries and show the same respect for his children as you do for yours, or does he put them on the backburner when he's dating? Does he maintain a close relationship with them, or has he drifted, emotionally or physically? I have met several men who have chosen to move states away or even across the country from where their children live. Their rationale behind this abandonment has run the gamut: "Their mother won't let me see them anyway," "We have never been close," "I still get him all summer," "I couldn't pass up the job opportunity," and the good ol' avoidance standby, "It's a long story." But here's the thing: I was recently offered eleven different leadership positions within eighteen months, and I turned them all down because I will never leave my children. There is no one, no opportunity, and no situation that would cause me to abandon my children and not see them as much as possible. If a man is easily swayed to leave his own child, then how easily will he find reasons to leave you and your children in the future? In other words, how conditional is his love?

When a man understands and respects that your children come first, he will show it from the beginning. Watch, he will want to know your custody schedule. He will want to know when you are available. He will respect your time with your children. This is very important! When a man is emotionally stable and respects your relationship with your children, he will not interrupt your time with them. You'll be able to tell early too. Does he monopolize your time with text messages and phone calls when he knows you have your children or get upset when you have to change your plans with him to accommodate them? Remember, he will only be as respectful as you command. So keep putting your children first, and if he's worth your time, he'll take the hint.

It's also important to keep an eye on how and when he makes time for you, even if he does respect the boundaries you've set around the kids. If his only solution is to come visit you when the children have gone to bed, what does that say about how he values you? Is this real, quality time, or is he merely attempting to shoplift the pootie? Are you allowing it? As a single man at the gym once told me (very unnecessarily, I might add), "Without a doubt, if a man is asking to come over after nine o'clock at night, it is only for one reason." Ladies, we should always be on the lookout for patterns that indicate red flags in a new relationship, but when our children are involved it is more important than ever to pay attention to the signs of a shoplifter!

WHEN TO INTRODUCE YOUR KIDS

Introducing someone to your children is the most personal thing you can do in a relationship. This event has all the weight of meeting your boyfriend's parents when you were eighteen, except that now you're responsible for the impact this person has on your children. No pressure! I learned quickly how much this could affect my children.

204

For example, after being single for approximately six months I started seeing someone I'd gone to high school with. I hadn't known this person well in school, nor did I recognize them twenty years later, but let me tell you, he was *hot!* I mean, he looked like he came straight off of a GQ magazine cover! We dated casually for about four weeks until one day he called and dropped the infamous, "We need to talk." The thoughts running through my head were, *"Oh great, what did I do this time?" "You screwed this one up!"* and *"Yep, he's canning you!"* When he got to my house, we sat on the couch, and he proceeded to tell me he was a registered sex offender! What the hell? How does this happen to me? This is why you do not introduce people to your children, and thank God I hadn't! Incidentally, this was also the moment I started investigating people thoroughly enough to make the FBI proud before I went out with them.

When it's time to think about introducing a partner to your children, it's important to put your kids' feelings first, recognizing that this may not be quite as joyful for them as it is for you. Do you think your children are thinking, *"I can't wait to have a stepparent!"?* As a child who grew up with divorced parents, I can help answer that: no. There is no child who desires to have a stepparent. Children desire their own parents, and any substitute is a threat to the perfect world they've created in their minds. Despite how much you may crave a life partner in parenting, that ship has sailed. No matter how perfect your new relationship, no one can replace a parent in a child's eyes.

So when is it time to make introductions? There are women I know who introduce their children to men after one or two dates. I went out with a man once who had his own twist on the infamous "three date rule." After three dates, if he was still interested in you, he introduced you to his children. Let's be real clear: this was all about shoplifting the pootie! And to make matters worse, he was using his children as leverage! Too many times, adults put their physical desires over the well-being of their children. Let's just say, Mr. Three Date Rule and I didn't see each other after three dates. Remember, in order for me to desire you, I must respect you. There is not, and there cannot be, a hard and fast number of dates that indicates it's time to introduce the children. In the book *I Can't Believe You Went Through My Stuff! How to Give Your Teens the Privacy They Crave and the Guidance They Need*, Dr. Peter Sheras explains that it's the level of commitment to the relationship, rather than the duration, that's important in deciding when to introduce children. Before a man meets your children, he is merely a guy you are dating. When a man meets your children, he is becoming family. You have had the DTR chat, you have laid out the pillars, and he has exceeded your expectations. And there is no limit on how long it can or should take to get to that point. I know an amazing PowerMom who has been in a committed relationship for almost three years, and her partner did not meet the children until year two. Everyone's timing is different, and what is important is the commitment to the relationship as opposed to the calendar date.

Does this mean your children never see you going on dates at all, until one day you show up completely in love? Not necessarily. As I've talked with women who were raised by single women, they've all smiled as they've recalled watching their mothers get ready for dates. It is good and natural for our children to see that we play more roles than mom and that we are romantically desired by others. This is a very fine line that can be controversial among single parents, but I try to be open with my children about my dating life, because I want to show them an example of healthy dating that they could possibly want to model.

If you're tempted to introduce your kids to each man who calls and texts, reflect on why you think that is. What would be the purpose? Who would benefit, and how? Are you tempted to make introductions out of convenience? Do *you* want them to meet him, or do your children want to meet that person? Who sets the standards? You, your children, or the person you are dating? Your children are very fragile and emotionally immature beings, and they will not be able to handle meeting all the people you encounter in your dating life. (Let's be real: sometimes I have trouble handling all those people myself!) If your children become attached to the men you are dating and the relationships do not work out, are you prepared to continually nurture your children through your breakups? The more partners that come in and out of our children's lives, the more feelings of instability and abandonment they're likely to experience. Studies have shown that this impacts all areas of a child's life and may even reopen past divorce wounds. It is our job as parents to filter this hurt from our children's lives.

The "right time" to introduce the children will be different for every woman and every relationship, and only you can determine the criteria. But no matter what, remember that *you* set the standards, *you* protect your children, and *you* say when it's okay to make introductions. Any man who complains about or does not understand this mindset is not ready to date a PowerMom. A man of worth will be patient, court you, and befriend your children when the time is right.

You and your children become who you surround yourselves with. The people you introduce your children to will directly impact the way they live. When we allow people into our lives who have certain habits and behaviors, we are showing our children those behaviors are ok, and they will begin to emulate what they see. Do you include your children at a dinner party where you can model etiquette and thoughtful conversation, or do you bring them to the club and model a party lifestyle? Once I started realizing how impactful this phenomenon truly is, I started asking myself, "Is he someone I want to influence my child?" before deciding whether to accept a date. If there was anything that held me back, then I needed to walk away. I had to decide if my potential partners' habits would have the right influence on my children.

How does being a mom define your dating life?
How is your model of dating defining you as a mother?
What type of commitment do you need in order to
introduce someone to your children?
What do you want your children to remember
about your dating life as adults?
How do you expect your partner to also court your children?

BIG DISCUSSIONS TO HAVE EARLY

I can only imagine that dating without children involves a very different mindset. The questions and conversation I have with men would probably not occur until much later in the process if I were not a mother.

If a man has children, I want to know how he parents them. How involved is he in their lives? Time usually reveals this, but upfront conversations can be very enlightening. Every parent loves their children, but do they love the same way you do? If a man and I are not in alignment in how we parent, it makes a relationship very difficult. I have found that, when many of the other pillars align, this pillar tends to fall into place very easily. When someone shows you his priorities in life, believe him. If he works all the time, know that won't change. If he exercises all the time, that is a priority in his life. What about the guy who chooses to leave his children and move across the country? It is difficult for someone to understand that you are prioritizing your children when they have never prioritized their own. Parenting alignment is so important, especially while the children live at home.

I had another man from high school reach out and ask me to go have a cup of coffee. I hadn't seen him in more than twenty years, and we had a great time reminiscing and catching up. Then I learned that he had left his children and former spouse in California. He said his reason for leaving was that he was unhappy in his job and his city. He told me stories of his children calling him, crying and begging to see him. It made my stomach turn, but it didn't seem to faze him. I could barely be without my children for the weekend, much less months at a time. We were not in alignment regarding parenting priorities. I was obviously willing to sacrifice whatever it took to be with my children, but his children were hardly more than an afterthought for him. I thanked him for coffee and let him know we needed to just be friends.

Another big topic I hit on early is whether a man desires to have children of his own if he doesn't already or more children if he does. Do you desire more children? Are you physically able to conceive more children? Perhaps most importantly, do you really want to change more diapers?! You must know whether you and a potential partner are in agreement on these issues before dipping into the dating pond. Men have the same desires and joys around parenthood that women do, and to take away this joy from another is not fair. I have experienced this extreme pain and desire in my life, and I know just how raw it is. If you don't want any more children, you must be very direct about your desires and expectations before your emotional connection is strong enough to get in the way. Darlin' nothing is coming out of this oven ever again! Your genes will never run around this world paired with mine! (And no, I will not adopt. I do not need or want to change more diapers, and I really value sleep.) But to rob someone *else* of the parenthood journey—and strictly by not having a conversation—would be one of the biggest injustices I could impose on another.

Alternatively, if you *do* want more children, be direct about that too. You would never want to force children on someone who doesn't want them, but there is no need to sacrifice your dream for a potential partner either. If he doesn't want kids, someone else will come along soon enough who may feel differently.

It's so important to have this conversation very early on—possibly even before you ever go out with a man. I mean, if you're not in sync, what's the point? They may want children, but this doesn't mean they want *your* children! And you may not want theirs. I had accepted a dinner invitation from a man, but as we continued chatting, I learned he had a small child in diapers. Whoa! Dinner was at a very nice restaurant in town, but I cancelled anyway, because I was not prepared to have a baby in my life. I had moved past diapers, and I wasn't going back. I didn't want to waste his time or money, nor did I want to waste mine!

There are so many conversations to have about dating with children, and these can be particularly emotional. Coming from curiosity rather than judgment in all scenarios fosters open conversation and brings enormous clarity. What is most important is how you raise your children, and how involved are you asking a potential partner to be? Do you share the same discipline practices, or does one partner believe in spanking children while the other is against it? Is faith part of your parenting, and what does it look like if one of you is Christian and the other is Agnostic? How will you parent together with these polarizing priorities?

Education is another big question, and it boils down to how each of you envisions raising future adults. What are your views on private versus public education? Supporting children through college versus asking them to take out loans? What about graduate school? I once met a PowerDad who co-parented and home-schooled his children with his ex-wife. The children were the priority for all parties, as they should be, but his specific parenting practices, mindsets, and choices were not in alignment with mine, so the relationship never progressed. How do you both intend to educate, influence, and make choices for your children, and are those philosophies in alignment? Do you both have the same expectations for your children's futures, and how are you making parenting choices to guide them?

To hold the title of mother means to care for and protect your children. They came into your life before any new partner or mate, and they will always come first. It isn't always easy, but in the long run, you'll waste less time dating people who don't understand your values or priorities if you're clear about them up front and you cut those who don't understand. We only have eighteen summers with our children before they "leave the nest," and when we share that limited time with anyone else, it should only be when their parenting views align with ours.

Holding Your Standards High

After selling property for over eighteen years, I've noticed a pattern when the market is tight and inventory is low. People will present a wish list of what they are looking for in a property, but it won't be easy to find right away. Some buyers will start to settle due to being anxious and ready to move. But inevitably, if they are patient enough to stick it out, the property that is their perfect fit presents itself.

In dating, it is also easy to create your list of standards, become frustrated with the market, and settle. Unfortunately, doing so will ultimately cause you to repeat your damaging patterns. Though the dating market may seem bleak, I continue to observe people being patient, staying true to their standards, and finding the right partner at the right moment.

Each date, each conversation, and each interaction with a man in my singlehood has taught me a lesson. I have learned what I desire and do not desire largely by seeing those things in others through the journey. If it were not for the heartbreaks, I would not have the insight into what I need in a relationship. If I had not encountered amazing qualities in some and less desirable qualities in others, then I wouldn't be able to recognize them in the next man who crosses my path.

To be able to have conversations with other men and women who were in the Singlehood, who struggled and found loving life partners, gives me hope and encouragement. When we see others in life who possess the qualities we desire, it affirms that what we desire is possible and gives us the hope we need to stay vigilant in our pursuit of partnership by upholding our standards and maintaining our worth. Cultivating a tribe to encourage and uplift you through the trials of life is priceless, and the gratitude to be found there is immeasurable. Once you do that, the Singlehood will merely be a state of mind, because your tribe will always be with you.

How we choose to frame our past experiences will determine the outcome of future jaunts in the journey. If we choose to see the good and learn from the mistakes we and others in the Singlehood have made, then we will maintain our hope and gratitude. Sometimes, we'll even realize the joy single life has to offer, and we'll thank those who helped us arrive in the Singlehood.

Many times, hope and gratitude are what get us through the Singlehood. There are amazing people in this world who want the same things in life as we do. Several men have reminded me of that, and it is always so refreshing! Seeing the hope in your interactions with others helps us maintain positivity and focus on what is important: knowing there are those out there who do align with us and will sustain us and our standards. We as PowerWomen—and PowerMen too—must encourage one another through the Singlehood by modeling standards and self-worth in order to provide hope for the future. Remember, the right partner will arrive at the perfect time.

When you discover your value proposition, settle into your happiness within the Singlehood, and discern your dating standards, then your joy in the dating space will be abundant. You will have the time of your life, and laughter will consume your calendar. Discover your own value, and identify what brings you joy, then start to see those things in others and bathe in the joy of your singlehood journey! How are you finding gratitude in your singlehood?

About the Author

Claire Brown is a divorced mother of two who has been dating—successfully or unsuccessfully, depending on which date she's talking about—since 2015. Because she married young, she had to discover who she was and what she wanted in the dating world after she divorced. She had to define her standards. To find connection and support from other women in her personal and professional life, she created the PowerWomen platform.

Claire runs a successful real estate team, coaches executives, hosts a podcast, mentors other women (and men) in her field, and is, above all, a proud PowerMom.

Join the public PowerWomen group on social media and, locally, the Little Rock PowerWomen or NWA PowerWomen groups. If you are interested in starting a group in your area, let us know. We'd love to talk about how we can franchise with you!

www.thepowerwomen.com
https://www.facebook.com/PowerWomenRise/

Endnotes

1 Friday, Francesca. "More Americans Are Single Than Ever Before-And They're Healthier, Too." *Observer*, January 16, 2018. https://observer.com/2018/01/more-americans-are-single-than-ever-before-and-theyre-healthier-too/.

2 Webb, Amy. TEDSalon NY2013. TEDTalks, 2013. https://www.ted.com/talks/amy_webb_how_i_hacked_online_dating/transcript?language=en.

3 Harrington, Rebecca. "One Parent Behavior May Affect Kids of Divorce More than Divorce Itself." *Business Insider*. Business Insider, May 23, 2016. https://www.businessinsider.com/children-of-divorce-odds-of-divorcing-2016-5.

4 "How Fathers Influence Their Daughters' Romantic Relationships." Institute for Family Studies, July 15, 2019. https://ifstudies.org/blog/how-fathers-influence-their-daughters-romantic-relationships.

5 "Quick Real Estate Statistics." www.nar.realtor, May 11, 2018. https://www.nar.realtor/research-and-statistics/quick-real-estate-statistics.

6 "In A New Memoir, Maya Angelou Recalls How A 'Lady' Became 'Mom'." *NPR*, March 27, 2013. https://www.npr.org/2013/03/31/175493858/in-a-new-memoir-maya-angelou-recalls-how-a-lady-became-mom.

7 Hasinoff, Amy Adele. "How to Practice Safe Sexting." TEDxMileHigh. TEDTalks, June 2016. https://www.ted.com/talks/amy_adele_hasinoff_how_to_practice_safe_sexting.

8 Dodgson, Lindsay. "A Psychologist Says You Should Actually Talk

about Exes on a First Date - Here's Why." *Business Insider*, March 7, 2018. https://www.businessinsider.com/its-fine-to-talk-about-exes-on-a-first-date-heres-why-2018-3.

9 "Dating Someone Who Doesn't Have Close Friends: Good or Bad Idea?" eHarmony, February 21, 2018. https://www.eharmony.com/dating-advice/dating-tips/dating-someone-who-doesnt-have-close-friends-good-or-bad-idea/

10 Pat Mitchell. "Becoming a Dangerous Woman - A Declaration and a New Book Title." May 20, 2019. https://www.patmitchellmedia.com/journal/2019/5/20/becoming-a-dangerous-woman-declaration-book-title.

11 Gourani, Soulaima. "Women: Know Your Value." *Forbes Magazine*, March 8, 2019. https://www.forbes.com/sites/soulaimagourani/2019/03/07/women-know-your-value/#13364a1145cf.

12 "What Is the Rape Kit Backlog?" endthebacklog.org. http://www.endthebacklog.org/backlog/what-rape-kit-backlog.

13 Tuttle, Brad. "Sex Keeps Getting Cheaper Around the Globe." Money, August 12, 2014. https://money.com/sex-prices-prostitutes-cheap/.

14 Rachel Morgan and Grace Kena. "Criminal Victimization, 2016: Revised." U.S. Department of Justice, October 2018.

15 "Victims of Sexual Violence: Statistics." RAINN. https://www.rainn.org/statistics/victims-sexual-violence.

16 Dietrich, Catherine. "To the 30-Something Moms." *HuffPost*, July 13, 2017. https://www.huffpost.com/entry/to-the-30-something-moms_b_10948354.

17 Mayer, John. 2017. "If you're pretty, you're pretty; but the only way to be beautiful is to be loving. Otherwise, it's just "congratulations about your face." Twitter, October 19, 2017, 1:45 p.m. https://twitter.com/JohnMayer/status/921085014607056896

18 Pew Research Center, "One in Five U.S. Adults Were Raised in Interfaith Homes," October 26, 2016, based on the 2014 Religious Landscape Study, https://www.pewforum.org/2016/10/26/religion-

in-marriages-and-families/.

19 Amy Webb, "How I Hacked Online Dating," TED Talk / TEDSalon NY2013, April 2013, https://www.ted.com/talks/amy_webb_how_i_hacked_online_dating?language=en#t-512295

20 Garcia, Justin R., Chris Reiber, Sean G. Massey, and Ann M. Merriwether. "Sexual Hookup Culture: A Review." *Review of General Psychology* 16, no. 2 (2012): 161–76. https://doi.org/10.1037/a0027911.

21 Hillin, Taryn. "Study Finds Why People Stay In Bad Relationships." *HuffPost*, January 23, 2014. https://www.huffpost.com/entry/fear-of-being-alone-study_n_4387157.

22 Hoffower, Hillary. "More Couples Are Taking on Debt to Have Instagram-Worthy Weddings. Here's How Much It Costs to Get Married in the US." *Business Insider*, July 26, 2019. https://www.businessinsider.com/how-much-does-it-cost-to-get-married-average-wedding-2019-7.

23 Dorothy Tennov, *Love and Limerence: The Experience of Being in Love*, Scarborough House, 1998.

24 Hussar, Daniels. "The Truth About Your Sexual Peak." *Women's Health*, October 22, 2019. https://www.womenshealthmag.com/sex-and-love/a19983455/sexual-peaks/.

25 Emma Johnson, "Dating Coach: 'Single Moms Are Hot on the Successful-Men Market.'" Wealthysinglemommy.com, January 16, 2020. https://www.wealthysinglemommy.com/dating-expert-single-moms-are-hot-on-the-successful-men-market/.

26 Kale, Sirin. "The Life of the Skin-Hungry: Can You Go Crazy from a Lack Of Touch?" *Vice*, November 8, 2016. https://www.vice.com/en_us/article/d3gzba/the-life-of-the-skin-hungry-can-you-go-crazy-from-a-lack-of-touch.

27 "The Surprising Truth About Modern Hook-Ups." *Psychology Today*. Sussex Publishers. Accessed February 11, 2020. https://www.psychologytoday.com/us/blog/all-about-sex/201602/the-surprising-truth-about-modern-hook-ups.

28 Ryan, Ronnie Ann. "The 3 Biggest Dating Dealbreakers For Those Over 50." *HuffPost*, October 5, 2013. https://www.huffpost.com/entry/dating-dealbreakers_n_4032034.

29 "Authenticity (Philosophy)." Wikipedia. Wikimedia Foundation, December 22, 2019. https://en.wikipedia.org/wiki/Authenticity_ (philosophy).

30 Krotz, Joanna. "Queen Bee Syndrome: Do Women Judge Women Leaders More Harshly?" NAFE, December 20, 2018. https://www.nafe.com/queen-bee-syndrome-do-women-judge-women-leaders-more-harshly.

31 Josephs, Lawrence. "Why Authenticity Is the Best Dating Strategy." *Psychology Today*. Sussex Publishers, March 2, 2019. https://www.psychologytoday.com/us/blog/between-the-sheets/201903/why-authenticity-is-the-best-dating-strategy.

32 "Breastfeeding Information." La Leche League USA. Accessed February 12, 2020. https://lllusa.org/bfinfo/.

33 Meeussen, Loes, and Colette Van Laar. "Feeling Pressure to Be a Perfect Mother Relates to Parental Burnout and Career Ambitions." *Frontiers in Psychology*. Frontiers Media S.A., November 5, 2018. https://www.ncbi.nlm.nih.gov/pmc/articles/PMC6230657/.

34 Microsoft 2020 Super Bowl Commercial: Be The One / Katie Sowers. Microsoft, 2020. https://www.microsoft.com/inculture/people-who-inspire/katie-sowers-nfl-coach/.

35 Brown, Brené, "The Power of Vulnerability," TEDxHouston. TEDTalks, June 2010. https://www.ted.com/talks/brene_brown_the_power_of_vulnerability.

36 Meltzer, Marisa. "How to Avoid a Romance Scam When Using Online Dating Sites." *Consumer Reports*. Accessed February 12, 2020. https://www.consumerreports.org/dating-relationships/online-dating-romance-scams/.

37 Konish, Lorie. "Women Are More Likely to Leave Financial Planning to Their Spouses. Here's Why That's a Problem." CNBC, March 18, 2019. https://www.cnbc.com/2019/03/18/women-are-more-likely-

to-leave-money-decisions-to-their-spouses.html.

38 Orman, Suze. "Women and Money." Women and Money (podcast), September 15, 2019. https://omny.fm/shows/suze-ormans-women-and-money/the-money-mind.

39 Rea, Jamie. "The Number One Reason People Get Back With Their Exes." The Good Men Project, November 10, 2017. https://goodmenproject.com/sex-relationships/number-one-reason-people-get-back-exes-cmtt/.

40 Bach, Deborah. "Is Divorce Seasonal? UW Research Shows Biannual Spike in Divorce Filings." UW News. University of Washington, August 21, 2016. https://www.washington.edu/news/2016/08/21/is-divorce-seasonal-uw-research-shows-biannual-spike-in-divorce-filings/.

41 Manson, Mark. "Every Successful Relationship Is Successful for the Same Exact Reasons." Mark Manson, October 8, 2019. https://markmanson.net/relationship-advice.

42 Firestone, Lisa. "The Unselfish Art of Prioritizing Yourself." Psychology Today, August 17, 2017. https://www.psychologytoday.com/us/blog/compassion-matters/201708/the-unselfish-art-prioritizing-yourself.

43 Holland, Kimberly. "Identifying and Managing Abandonment Issues." Healthline, February 21, 2019. https://www.healthline.com/health/mental-health/abandonment-issues#how-to-help.

44 Hartwell-Walker, Marie. "What To Do About Attention-Seeking Kids." Psych Central, October 8, 2018. https://psychcentral.com/lib/what-to-do-about-attention-seeking-kids/.

Made in the USA
Columbia, SC
30 July 2021

42673123R00140